BRIGHAM YOUNG

the

Man of the Hour

by

Leah D. Widtsoe

BOOKCRAFT

SALT LAKE CITY, UTAH

$15.00

FOREWORD

It was 1846. A man of the hour was needed!

Neighboring communities, livid with jealous, bloody hate, supported by guns and arson, by the governor and other state officials, had driven the Latter-day Saints from their homes and all their possessions, with the warning that they must leave their native country. This the people had endured before, time and time again. Now a whole people, nearly twenty thousand, were left homeless and friendless. And this after years of unspeakable persecution! It was a crisis unequaled in the history of civilization.

The suffering expatriates, though full of faith, asked anxious questions: Whither should they go? How should they travel? Could they regain their prosperity? Was there left on earth a place of peace for them and their children?

Then the appointed leader, Brigham Young, made answer. He led them over plains, mountains and deserts, into the inhospitable, unoccupied region of the Great Basin of North America. From the shores of the Great Salt Lake as a center, to the wonder and applause of the world, he founded on the desert a successful commonwealth, in which peace reigned. In this achievement he laid bare, also, for the world's good, the eternal principles of successful governments among men.

It is a breath-taking, heartwarming story, seldom if ever equaled in the annals of struggling man. Faith, courage, adventure and romance sparkle from facets of pioneer aspiration, endeavor and endurance. Brigham Young, by common consent, has found his place among the great ones of the earth. At his birthplace, an admirer has carved on a marble slab that Brigham Young was

a man of "great courage and superb endowment." And so he was!

In this book, adapted from an earlier Mutual Improvement study course, the captivating story of Brigham Young's life and achievements is told, with historical accuracy, yet with such sympathetic skill that flesh-and-blood life is given to the great pioneer. His own words often tell the story. Though the pages are fewer—deliberately done for our hurrying age—everything vital in the man's life has been preserved, and the thrill of the soul-stirring events of the times retained.

The author, herself a granddaughter, and biographer with her mother in a larger volume of Brigham Young ("The Life of Brigham Young," Susa Y. Gates and Leah D. Widstoe) is fully qualified for the task she has set herself—to tell comprehensively and understandingly, yet briefly, the life of the founder of the intermountain west of America.

This is a valuable, readable, interesting addition to the biographical literature about the humble "painter and glazier," who rose to world-wide fame because of his world-wide service.

JOHN A. WIDTSOE

TABLE OF CONTENTS

CHRONOLOGY OF THE EVENTS IN THE LIFE OF BRIGHAM YOUNG

1801—June 1st, Born at Whittingham, Vermont.

1824—Married Miriam Works.

1832—April 14, Baptized into the Church.

1832—His wife Miriam died.

1833—Moved to Kirtland, Ohio.

1834—Married Mary Ann Angell.

1834—Took part in journey of Zion's Camp.

1835—Important missionary assignment.

1835—Ordained an Apostle.

1837—Moved from Kirtland to Missouri.

1838—Removed Saints from Missouri to Illinois.

1838—Settled in Nauvoo, Illinois.

1839—Went on a mission to England.

1844—As president of the Council of Twelve, became the leader of the Church.

1846—The Nauvoo Temple was dedicated.

1846—Left Nauvoo for the West.

1847—Led Pioneer company to the Salt Lake Valley.

1847—Sustained as President of the Church.

1849—Elected Governor of the "Provisional State of Deseret."

1850—Appointed Governor of the Territory of Utah.

1850—Founded University of Deseret (now Utah).

1852—Social Hall was built.

1853—The cornerstone for the Salt Lake Temple was laid.

1857—Entrance of Johnston's Army, and another Governor of Utah appointed.

1862—Salt Lake Theatre was built.

1865—Deseret Telegraph Company established.

1867—The Salt Lake Tabernacle was dedicated.

1875—The cornerstone of the Manti Temple was laid.

1875—Founded Brigham Young Academy (now University).

1877—Founded Brigham Young College at Logan.

1877—Dedicated St. George Temple.

1877—Cornerstone of Logan Temple was laid.

1877—August 27, Died in Salt Lake City.

REFERENCES

A list of references to quotations given in the text will be found on pages 180 to 184.

CHAPTER I.

INTRODUCING THE MAN OF THE HOUR

THE study of history or biography is stimulating to the extent that the lessons learned from such study may be applied to the affairs of daily life, and the enrichment of one's character. While the material world changes from age to age, the problems of human advancement or retrogression remain fairly constant. Therefore, a study of the past, if it is to be really worth-while, should help the reader to live a richer life in applying the wisdom or avoiding the mistakes of the one whose life is being reviewed. In that sense the study of a historical character may become a guide or an inspiration for more worth-while life today.

The man whose life is here briefly told was greatly beloved by his own people, feared and hated by his enemies, yet withal was one of the greatest characters of the nineteenth century. He possessed a fine physique, a keen mind, with a sturdy, lovable character fashioned by the severe yet upbuilding forces of pioneer life, tempered by his Christian parentage and wholesome environment.

A most interesting fact concerning the early founders of this state is that most of them were descendants of loyal patriots who helped in the founding and building of the United States of America. No finer heritage may be claimed by any United States citizen than that which belongs to the founders of Mormonism. Like Nephi of old they might one and all have begun their life narrative by saying, "Having been born of goodly parents."

Men are usually conceded to be largely what heredity and environment make of them. To this, of course, must be added the personal equation of each individual as influenced by the exercise of his own will and other latent powers. So, Brigham Young is herewith presented to you.

Brigham's progenitors were typical Americans and Puritans. William Young, the earliest known progenitor, between 1720 and 1730 was a worshipper at the old South Church in Boston, Massachusetts, where his older children were christened. In 1721 he went north with a company of adventurers into new lands, into Barrington and Nottingham, New Hampshire, to settle on the Lamphrey River. The New Hampshire County History says: "These towns were settled by men, or children of men, who had shown faithfulness and bravery in the Indian wars. These lands were given these men by the Government in recognition of this service." William Young, Brigham's great grandfather, from this showing as well as from his will, was a man of considerable means and influence. He later removed to Hopkinton, Massachusetts.

William's son Joseph Young was born about 1739. He married, August 27, 1759, Mrs. Elizabeth Hayden Treadway, a widow with four children. Joseph's children are Susanna, William, John, Joseph, Anna and Ichabod —John being the father of Brigham.

In the opening years of the nineteenth century, there was a restless, migratory movement of the new citizens of the recently established United States of America. Especially was this true of soldiers who had served in the Revolutionary War. Contact with settlers in other localities had opened up to New England pioneer eyes the desirability and the handicaps of various sections along the Eastern seaboard. This family of Youngs, one of many with like surname and no known kinship, had felt the adventurous urge, and had moved into the more sparsely settled regions of Vermont. There, in the small town of Whittingham, Windham County, on June 1, 1801, Brigham Young was born.

Brigham's mother, Abigail Howe, was a lovable and superior woman. Most great men accord their mothers much credit for their life accomplishment—so it was with Brigham.

In the manuscript history of Brigham Young by his daughter, Susa Young Gates, is given a picture of her character and life. "Abigail or 'Nabby' was one of five sisters, all of whom were pretty, while Abigail was said to be the most beautiful woman in the country. She had blue eyes, yellowish brown hair, which waved gracefully across her brow. She and her sisters were all singers and many social affairs were brightened by these girls singing old English madrigals and hymns with their sweet natural voices. Abigail was greatly beloved by all her friends and associates, and was said by Aunt Maria Burton to be quite a neighborhood reformer.

"Married when nineteen years of age, 'Nabby' followed the pioneer fortunes of her restless husband, John Young, bearing children by the wayside, in hastily built log houses, leaving one home after another, treking from Hopkinton, Massachusetts, with eight little children to Vermont; then after the birth of her ninth child, Brigham Young, turning south again; this time to Auburn, New York, then in two years over to Smyrna, New York, and from there to Cayuga County at Genoa, where they lived for some years.

"Always patient, loving and tender, she sang her songs of love and faith over the cradles of her babies, at the moving hearthstone of wagon or cabin. She was also a choir singer in the Methodist congregations where she and her God-fearing husband worshipped. Abigail's sons inherited her musical talent. The father, John Young, and his sons were also fine singers and often sang in private and public.

"Nabby was exquisitely neat in her ways, refined in speech and character, a reader and a student of human nature; and bequeathed to her children her own loyal devotion to truth and duty, to God and country—all of which made her home blessed, whether in wilderness or village. Gifted, lovely, noble she was, according to all who knew her. She was an invalid for some years, but she would be invited to visit her friends, especially young couples just starting out in life and would be sent for to spend the day in instructing and advising them how to avoid the many pitfalls of married life.

"The social-religious life of the Young family, which marked Brigham's boyhood and youth, was like that of other New Englanders, a constant scene of healthy struggle with the forces of physical and human nature. Sabbath worship, singing-schools, quilting, apple bees, corn-huskings, barn-raisings, weddings, and even funerals, were the diversions which varied the grinding toil and gave scope and opportunity for social mingling and informal gaiety."

A **personal estimate of his forebears** was expressed by Brigham in his maturity. They were strict yet superior people and his own memory of them will help to give a better understanding of their descendants. He says: "My grandfather, Joseph Young, was a physician and surgeon in the French and Indian Wars. He was killed by the fall of a pole from a fence in the year 1769.

"My father, John Young, was born March 7, 1763, in Hopkinton, Middlesex County, Massachusetts. He was from his boyhood very circumspect, exemplary and religious, and was from an early period of his life a member of the Methodist Church. At the age of seventeen, he enlisted in the American Revolutionary War, and served under General Washington. He was in three campaigns in his own native state and New Jersey. In the year 1782, he married Abigail (Nabby) Howe, daughter of Phineas and Susanna, whose maiden name was Goddard. Nabby was born May 3, 1766 and died June 11, 1815 in Genoa, Cayuga County, New York. He moved from Hopkinton in January, 1801, to Wittingham, Windham County, Vermont, taking his family with him where he remained for three years, opening new farms. He moved to Auburn, New York, in 1805. My mother died June 11, 1815 and father soon moved again.

"My ancestors were some of the most strict religionists that lived upon the earth. You no doubt can say the same about yours. Of my mother—she that bore me—I can say, no better woman ever lived in the world than she was. I have the feelings of a son towards her; I should have them—it is right; but I judge the matter pertaining to her from the principles and the spirit of the teachings I received from her.

"Would she countenance one of her children in the least act that was wrong according to her traditions? No, not in the least degree. I was brought up so strict, so firm in the faith of the Christian religion by my parents, that if I had said 'Devil,' I believed I had sworn very wickedly, no matter on what occasion or under what circumstances this might occur. If I used the name of Devil, I should have certainly been chastised, and that severely. Would my father or mother allow any of the children to say 'Darn it'? Were they ever allowed to say 'I vow'? No. If we said either of these words, we should have been whipped for it. I don't say that we did not say such things when out of the sight of Father and Mother; but if by any means it came to their ears, we were sure to be chastised.

"Did I ever hear a man swear in my father's house? No, never in my life. I never heard my father or any person about his premises swear as much as to say 'Darn it,' or 'Curse it,' or 'the Devil.' So you see I was brought up pretty strictly. My mother, while she lived, taught her children all the time to honor the name of the Father and the Son, and to reverence the holy Book. She said, read it, observe its precepts, and apply them to your lives as far as you can; do every thing that is good; do nothing that is evil; and if you see any persons in distress, administer to their wants; never suffer anger to arise in your bosoms; for, if you do, you may be overcome by evil. I do not know that I ever wronged my neighbor, even to the value of a pin. I was taught, when a child, not to take a pin from the door-yard of a neighbor, but to carry it into the house and give it to some of the family. Never did my mother or father countenance any of their children in anything to wrong their neighbor or fellow-being, even if they were injured by them. If they have injured me, says my father, let me return good for evil, and leave it in the hand of the Lord; he will bless me for doing right and curse them for doing wrong."[1]

Thus it may be seen how the forces of heredity, with a rather harsh pioneer environment, combined to make possible this "man of destiny."

As a young man, he was serious and industrious but gave little promise of the great destiny which awaited him. His powers of observation were very acute, and he had a keen sense of humor. He loved work, and valued the discipline of its steady, well-regulated demands. He says: "At an early age I labored with my father, assisting him to clear new land and cultivate his farm, passing through many hardships and privations incident to settling a new country."

Inheriting a love of harmony and beauty, he translated it into his daily task of developing beauty of line in bits of the homely furniture which he fashioned, in the planting of flowers about his cottage door, and in carefully planning the houses which he built. Beauty of trees, harmony of color and line in valley and glade appealed to him rather in terms of human development than in pure esthetics. He loved nature as it contributed to man's comfort and growth.

He was a well-built man, about five feet ten inches tall, and was rather fair in complexion, with blue eyes and light brown hair. He was scrupulously clean in word, speech and act. Pope's phrase, that cleanliness is akin to godliness, would have seemed scripture to him. His personality was of the pervasive type. He was even-tempered and serene, and was quite incapable of an emotional cyclone, for his poised mind considered every future act and its consequences. He was decidedly social in his nature and thought well of men, having a keen appraisment of human values. In fact, while he studied the scriptures and politics, he studied men more. In return he was highly respected, and his close friends were men of superior native powers.

Brigham was certainly not a covetous man. Envy and jealousy, those egoistic attributes of small minds and selfish hearts, found no quarter in the large chamber of his soul. He was thrifty, farsighted and prudent. But all the after years of his life proved his incapability to hoard selfishly, to encroach on others or to profit through another man's loss. Accumulate means and property he did, but all that he gathered he used to make his family and his people happy and comfortable. On one occasion he said: "Why am I driven from my possessions? Why am I persecuted, and forced to leave thousands and thousands of dollars' worth of property in Ohio, Missouri, and Illinois? Though I have never looked back upon it, it is ashes under my feet. I am in the hands of God. He gave it, and He took it away; and blessed be the name of the Lord."[2]

Opinions of others who knew him personally are most interesting. A letter written by his brother Lorenzo has this to say of him: "Brigham was a man of strictly moral habits as far as I ever knew. I do not think he was ever known to drink liquor or use profane language. He was very industrious and hard working. As to his faults, I never knew of anything in particular. I never knew of his having difficulty with his associates or his brothers or sisters.

"I cannot remember of anything special in his early life as to his choice of play. I could not say for I was not with him to know. He was slow to get angry. I never knew of his getting angry but once in his youthful days when I thought he was violent. After mother's death the family were separated and never lived together as a family afterwards."

Following is a choice view of him as expressed by a stranger, with a defense from one of his contemporaries and personal friends. This comes from the diary of Isaiah M. Coombs, one of the best loved teachers of early days, who lived in Payson, and is given by his daughter, Mrs. Ida Coombs Lund. Coombs says: "I received a good letter from my boyhood friend Dr. Dryden Rogers (a non-Mormon). He had received my last with a likeness of President Young enclosed and this is what he says about it:

" ' I esteem it very highly. I was surprised at the massiveness of the forehead indicating an intellectual battery seldom seen. The picture does not indicate the sensualism which he is charged with. No one can deny the goodness of heart he possesses. I simply think him honestly deceived. Probably a more intimate acquaintance might modify my opinion and you are aware of the sources from whence my premises are drawn.'

"In my answer of this date I say, 'I think a man of President Young's mental calibre safe from deception. I feel morally certain that if you knew him as I know him, if you could hear his voice you would acquit him of that suspicion. No! President Young is not only sincere, but he is right! He represents himself as being the mouth-piece of God to the human family and such he is! the opinion of the world to the contrary notwithstanding. People may be deceived by the seeing of the eye and the hearing of the ear, but the manifestations of the Spirit of God leave no room for doubt, no chance for deception.' "

A "Modern" views Brigham Young. The prophecy concerning Joseph Smith, that his name should be known for good or ill throughout the countries of earth, is equally true of his friend and follower Brigham Young. During Brigham's lifetime and today his name was either famous or infamous throughout the civilized world. However, his true worth as a great statesman and empire builder is being recognized by all fair-minded students of history.

The following letter from far-off Czecho-Slovakia gives a clear estimate of the man who pioneered the building of this Far-west. It is from a very well educated friend and convert to the Truth, Mrs. Emilie Hromatkova.

"Since I became acquainted with Mormonism I felt a great admiration for Brigham Young. I always admired Moses, who led the people of old Israel to Canaan. But he brought them to a land of 'milk and honey.' Brigham Young did more than Moses did—he made 'the desert blossom like a rose.' It was this wonderful fact that awakened my interest for Mormonism when I heard the first lecture about it by Brother Gaeth.

"When I had the lucky chance to meet you and Sister Widtsoe in Prague and go with you to the Karlstein, I did not know anything about your close relationship to that remarkable man. Otherwise the joy I had in being with you would have been still keener through the sensation of reality, that the presence of living persons gives to a dream . . . .

"When I learned that you have written a biography of Brigham Young, that is in possession of Sister Gaeth, I asked her to lend it to me, and she kindly did so. While reading it I got the idea to ask your permission to translate it into German. I wrote to Brother Gaeth, and he answered he was sure that you would have no objection to my doing so. So I began the work some weeks ago, and it makes me really happy. All those long lonesome winter evenings are now filled up with a task that gives me joy and distraction. I am just living with all those folks in the book, going through all their distress and adventures, laughing and weeping with them.

"I should like everybody to read this wonderful book. I can scarcely believe that men have so dry hearts and so little understanding not to find out its beauties and to try to come near to them . . ."

Verily is his name and fame known far and wide!

A brief glimpse of his life philosophy possibly will give a fairer estimate of his real character than the opinion of friends or dear ones. He says: "From the days of my youth, and I will say from the day that I came upon this stage of action to act for myself, there never was a boy, a man, either old or middle-aged, that ever tried to live a life more pure and refined than your humble servant. As I told my friend, I have tried to make myself a better man from the day of our first acquaintance to this. I have not infringed upon any law, or trod upon the rights of my neighbors; but I have tried to walk in the paths of righteousness, and live a humble life, that I might gain eternal happiness. I make bold to speak thus, though in the eastern world it is quite unpopular to speak of one's own praise; but since I have become a western man, I can make stump speeches."[3]

Such was Brigham Young as a man. After this brief introduction one may feel a deeper interest in his life of great achievement and real success. In every deed he measured up to all the requirements of a great man, one who became to his people and his state **The Man of the Hour.**

CHAPTER 2

BRIGHAM YOUNG'S GREAT SPIRITUAL CRISIS

E VERY sane person has some life philosophy to guide his daily actions; most men call it their religion. Blessed is the man whose religion includes faith in God and His Son Jesus Christ, and a sure knowledge of the road to happiness and success in this life as a preparation for life hereafter. A religion which teaches less than this is but fragmentary and can never be truly satisfying to the thinking mind.

Brigham Young was essentially a man of action, yet withal he had a deeply spiritual nature. He well understood that man is but a drifting, puny speck upon life's troubled waters without the safe anchorage of a sane and active faith in a Supreme Power. His mental outlook was such that dormant belief were useless unless it could be translated into daily participation in a program which proved his faith and gave it power to function. Therefore he felt that all men need religion, which to him was but a means of working out God's purpose with His mortal children.

Which of the various existing religions should he accept? This was a problem which gave him deep concern, for he was a thorough Bible student and desired the Truth. He says: "Before Joseph Smith made known what the Lord had revealed to him, before his name was even known among many of his neighbors, I knew that Jesus Christ had no true Church upon the earth. I read the Bible for myself; I was supposed to be an infidel and to content myself with a moral religion. When I was told to believe in Jesus Christ, and that was all that was required for salvation, I did not so understand the Bible. I understood from the Bible that when the Lord had a church upon the earth it was a system of ordinances, of laws and regulations to be obeyed, a society presided over and regulated by officers and ministers peculiar to itself to answer such and such purposes, and bring to pass such and such results, and I have not received a revelation to the contrary. Such a system answering the description given in the Bible I could not find on the earth, and I was not prepared to listen to the men who said 'lo here' and 'lo there,' who presented themselves, as they said, as true ministers of heaven. When I would ask the ministers of religion, if they were prepared to tell me how the kingdom of God should be built up; if that which is laid down in the New Testament is not the pattern, all the reply I could receive from them was: 'but you know my dear friend, that these things are done away.' They would tell me that ordinances were matters of ceremony, that belief in Jesus Christ was all-essential and all that was really necessary. I could only think of the religious world as a mass of confusion."[1]

"Before I embraced the Gospel, I understood pretty well what the different sects preached, but I was called an infidel because I could not embrace their dogmas. I could not believe all of Methodism, I could not believe all of the Baptists' doctrines; there were some things they preached I could believe and some I could not. I could not fully agree with the Presbyterians in their doctrines, nor with the Quakers, nor the Catholics, although they all have some truth. As far as their teachings were in accordance with the Bible, I could believe them, and no further. I was acquainted with the creeds of nearly all the various sects of dissenters in America, for I had made it my business to inquire into the principles in which they believed. I was religiously inclined in my youth, but I could not believe in their dogmas, for they did not commend themselves to my understanding though as a child I had attended their camp meetings, and had seen what they called the power of God. I had seen men and woman fall, and be as speechless and breathless as that stove before me. I had seen scientists hold the lightest feather they could procure at the nostrils and mouths of females to see if a particle of air passed to or from the lungs, and not a particle was discernible. When a child I saw all this, but I could not believe in their dogmas. I could not say the people were not sincere in their faith and acts, but it was all a mystery to me. I was not old enough, and did not understand enough to decide."[2]

"Before I heard the Gospel as again revealed in its purity through Joseph the Prophet, I was tolerably well acquainted with the spirit, disposition, tact, and talents possessed by the children of men; and though I was then but about thirty years of age, I had seen and heard enough to make me well acquainted with the people in their acts and dealings one towards another, the result of which was to make me sick, tired, and disgusted with the world; and had it been possible, I would have withdrawn from all people, except a few, who, like myself, would leave the vain, foolish, wicked, and unsatisfying customs and practices of the world. Sorrow, wretchedness, death, misery, disappointment, anguish, pain of heart, and crushed spirits prevail over the earth; and apparently, the whole of the intelligence of mankind is directed in a way to produce cruel and unnatural results."[3]

"What are the teachings of the Christian world? Many of you have had an experience among them, and can answer this question very well. I have had an experience in their midst, though I never bowed down to their creeds. I never could submit to their doctrines, for they taught that which was not in the Bible, and denied that which was found in the Bible, consequently I could not be a convert to their fanaticism. I am not today. In my youth I was called an infidel, and I was an infidel. What to? This Bible? No, to false creeds, and to professing without possessing. I did not believe in the sectarian religion, I could not see any utility in it, any further than a moral character was concerned, yet I believed the Bible. The natural wisdom and judgment which were given me from my youth, were sufficient to enable me to easily comprehend the discrepancies and lack in the creeds of the day."[4]

"Before I had made a profession of religion, I was thought to be an infidel by the Christians, because I could not believe their nonsense. Yet the secret feeling of my heart was that I would be willing to crawl around the earth on my hands and knees, to see such a man as was Peter, Jeremiah, Moses, or any man that could tell me anything about God, heaven, or the plan of salvation, so that I could pursue the path that leads to the kingdom of heaven."[5]

"I knew Methodism. The Methodist preachers used to talk with children in such a manner that I have often prayed, 'If there is a God in heaven, save me, that I may know all the truth and not be fooled by such doctrines.' I saw them 'get religion' all around me. Men were rolling and bawling and thumping but it had no effect on me. I wanted to know the truth that I might not be fooled. Children and young men 'got religion' but I could not get it till I was twenty-three years old; and then, in order to prevent my being pestered about it I joined Methodism."[6]

"I was a Bible reader before I came into this Church; and, so far as the letter of the Book was concerned, I understood it. I professed to be a believer in the Bible so far as I knew how; but as for understanding by the Spirit of the Lord, I never did until I became a Latter-day Saint."[7]

He hears the Truth. In the spring of 1829 Brigham moved with his family to Mendon, New York, which was about forty miles from Palmyra, where the family of the Prophet Joseph Smith lived.

A terse statement tells how the true gospel found its way into his life: "While I was living in Mendon there was printed in the newspaper a short paragraph; it was only about a square inch, but it stated that a young man had seen an angel who told him where to find an Indian Bible, and it went on to inquire what would happen if it should come forth; should we then know about the origin of the Indians? Soon after this the Book of Mormon was printed and came into our section of the country. The next spring I first saw the Book of Mormon, which Brother Samuel H. Smith brought and left with my brother-in-law, John P. Greene."[8]

Concerning the Book of Mormon he writes: "When the Book of Mormon was first printed, it came to my hands in two or three weeks afterwards. Did I believe, on the first intimation of it? The man that brought it to me, told me the same things; says he, 'This is the Gospel of salvation; a revelation the Lord has brought forth for the redemption of Israel; it is the Gospel; and according to Jesus Christ, and his Apostles, you must be baptized for the remission of sins, or you will be damned.' 'Hold on,' says I. The mantle of my traditions was over me to that degree, and my prepossessed feelings so interwoven with my nature, it was almost impossible for me to see at all; though I had beheld, all my life, that the traditions of the people was all the religion they had, I had got a mantle for myself. Says I, 'Wait a little while; what is the doctrine of the book, and of the revelations the Lord has given? Let me apply my heart to them'; and after I had done this, I considered it to be my right to know for myself, as much as any man on earth.

"I examined the matter studiously for two years before I made up my mind to receive that book. I knew it was true, as well as I knew that I could see with my eyes, or feel by the touch of my fingers, or be sensible of the demonstrations of any sense. Had not this been the case, I never would have embraced it to this day; it would have all been without form or comeliness to me. Yet I wished time sufficient to prove all things for myself."[9]

Brigham Young's approach to this most important subject is entirely according to what is termed in modern language the "scientific method." He listened to those who professed a knowledge of its truth; he studied it with all his power of mind and heart; he prayed about it; he weighed it in the balance of his past religious experience and found it **true!** Yet its acceptance needed more than earthly wisdom.

He explains that when he says: "If all the talent, tact, wisdom, and refinement of the world had been sent to me with the Book of Mormon, and had declared in the most exalted of earthly eloquence the truth of it, undertaking to prove it by learning and worldly wisdom, they would have been to me like the smoke which arises only to vanish away. But when I saw a man without eloquence, or talents for public speaking, who could only say, 'I know, by the power of the Holy Ghost, that the Book of Mormon is true, and that Joseph Smith

is a prophet of the Lord,' the Holy Ghost proceeding
from that individual illuminated my understanding, and
light, glory, and immortality were before me. I was
encircled by them, filled with them, and I knew for
myself that the testimony of the man was true. But the
wisdom of the world, I say again, is like smoke, like
the fog of the night, that disappears before the rays of
the luminary of day, or like the hoar-frost, in the
warmth of the sun's rays. My own judgment, natural
endowments, and education bowed to this simple but
mighty testimony. It filled my system with light and my
soul with joy. The world, with all its glory and gilded
show of its kings or potentates, sinks into perfect insig-
nificance, compared with the simple, unadorned testimony of the servant of God."[10]

He receives "the light." Brigham yearned for the
Truth, he needed it. Then came this new "great Light"
into his soul and he was sincere enough and wise enough
to recognize it.

He says regarding his final acceptance of Truth
restored: "I will inform you how I became a Mormon
—how the first solid impression was made upon my
mind. When I undertook to sound the doctrine of Mormonism I supposed I could handle it as I could the
Methodist, Prebyterian, and other creeds of Christendom,
which I had paid some considerable attention to, from the
first of my knowing anything about religion. When
Mormonism was first presented to me, I had not seen
one sect of religionists whose doctrines, from beginning
to end, did not appear to me like the man's masonry
which he had in a box, and which he exhibited for a
certain sum. He opened the main box from which he
took another box; unlocked that and slipped out another, then another, and another, and thus continued

to take box out of box until he came to an exceedingly small piece of wood; he then said to the spectators, 'That gentlemen and ladies, is free masonry.'

"I found all religions comparatively like this—they were so deficient in doctrine that when I tried to tie the loose ends and fragments together, they would break in my hands. When I commenced to examine Mormonism I found it impossible to take hold of either end of it; I found it was from eternity, passed through time, and into eternity again. When I discovered this, I said, 'It is worthy of the notice of man.' Then I applied my heart to wisdom, and sought diligently for understanding."[11]

His final testimony, after deep and serious study, came as he once related to his daughter, who asked him how she could know that Mormonism is true: "There is only one way to find out. And that is the way I found it out and the way your mother found it. Get down on your knees and ask God to give you that testimony and knowledge which Peter had when Christ asked the Apostles: 'Whom do ye say I am?' "[12]

Of his certain knowledge concerning the truth of the restored gospel he says: "I was brought up in the midst of Methodists, Episcopalians, Quakers and Presbyterians. But when Mormonism came along I fathomed it as far as I could and then I embraced it for all day long, that I might just live and die standing straight in this work."[13] The deep and sincere conversion of this good man can not be doubted.

Brigham Young recognized "his hour." He was baptized into the new Church, which is the restored Gospel of Jesus Christ, when he was in his thirty-first year and possessed of all the strength and virility of his young manhood. His conversion was not the result of an emotional cyclone, but came gradually during two years of deep study and prayer concerning it.

He tells of this event: "On April 14, 1832, I was baptized by Eleazer Miller, who confirmed me at the water's edge. We returned home, about two miles, the weather being cold and snowy; and before my clothes were dry on my back he laid his hands on me and ordained me an Elder at which I marvelled. According to the words of the Savior, I felt a humble, child-like spirit, witnessing unto me that my sins are forgiven."[14]

His conversion was of the mind and heart as well as of the spirit. From the day of his rebirth to the day of his death he never for one instant doubted the truth of the Gospel of Jesus Christ restored through the instrumentality of a modern prophet of God. Thus began a life of great activity and devotion to revealed Truth, and to the people who accepted it.

CHAPTER 3

HIS CONVERSION BECOMES ACTIVE

A DECISIVE test of the truth of any system of philosophy or religion is its power to be used daily and to enrich human life. If it cannot survive that test then it must be classed as man-made and must eventually go into the discard. A religion, if it is the true Gospel of Christ, must be applicable to every act of life and must concern man's entire well-being—yesterday and today, as well as throughout eternity.

Brigham Young's acceptance of the restored Gospel gave him a vision of its beauty and consistency as well as a knowledge of its eternal truth. Yet it were useless to him unless he could prove his joy in its possession by working for its spread among the people who so sadly needed its inspiring message. He said on one occasion: "This shouting and singing one's self away to everlasting bliss, may be all very well in its place, but this alone is folly to me; my religion is to know the will of God and do it."[1]

He had the deep satisfaction of having his dearly beloved wife accept the Truth just a few months prior to her death. He says: "About three weeks after my own baptism my wife was also baptised. This was in the town of Mendon, in Monroe county. I tarried during the summer preaching the Gospel in the regions round about, baptising and raising up churches"[2] (by which term he meant Branches of the Church).

Therefore one may say that his active ministry began from the time of his conversion. Through snow and ice he journeyed far and near to proclaim the "glad tidings" to all who would give ear. After the death of his wife he with his two little girls lived in the home of his nearest and dearest friend, Heber C. Kimball.

Sister Kimball's loving care of the motherless children enabled him to devote much of his time to the spread of the restored Gospel of Christ.

His loved ones were his first concern. Even before his own baptism, while he was considering and weighing the claims of the new-old Gospel of Jesus, he was trying to interest his father's family, for his four stalwart brothers and six sisters were near and dear to his heart. They, too, were made acquainted with the claims of the new Church and together and in groups they often discussed the "things pertaining to the kingdom."

He tells of his early efforts in their behalf: "Immediately after my return home from Pennsylvania I took my horse and sleigh and started to Canada after my brother, Joseph, taking my brother-in-law, John P. Greene, who was then on his way to his circuit, preaching the Methodist doctrine. We rode together as far as Sackett's Harbor. After finding my brother, Joseph, and explaining to him what I had learned of the Gospel in its purity, his heart rejoiced and he returned home with me, where we arrived in March."[3]

He was instrumental in bringing about finally the conversion and baptism of all his brothers and sisters, his father, as well as his own dying wife. Said he: "The Prophet could not come to our neighborhood then, so I preached to my family and related the truth about the Book of Mormon." He referred to this in a family gathering of Youngs, Havens, Howes, Goddards and Richards, held in Nauvoo, January 8, 1845: "Joseph (his elder brother), when he saw me believed the Book of Mormon. I preached to him first. And so I claim you all as the fruit of my labors. I am the first one of the family that embraced it understandingly."[4]

His father as well as his brothers Joseph and Phineas and sisters Fanny, Rhoda, Susanna and Louisa were all baptized in April, 1832. His youngest brother, Lorenzo, was baptized in September, 1832, while the eldest brother, John, waited till October, 1833.

That they were all truly converted is evidenced by the fact that they and their families went to Kirtland, there assisted in the building of the Temple and the City, and took an active part in the events which led the Prophet and his people from Kirtland, Ohio, to far West Missouri. The aged father died in Quincy, Illinois, in 1839, while the others went on to Nauvoo and finally to Utah where they and their large families remained faithful to the Gospel of Jesus Christ.

Because of bitter persecution, the Prophet had removed from New York State to a small village, Kirtland, near Cleveland, Ohio. Soon many of the early converts followed him and Kirtland became the first real headquarters of the new Church.

Brigham meets the Prophet. The greatest experience of Brigham's life to date was his meeting with the modern prophet of God.

He describes it thus: "In September, 1832, Brother Heber C. Kimball took his horses and wagon, Brother Joseph Young and myself accompanying him, and started for Kirtland to see the Prophet Joseph. We visited many friends on the way, and some branches of the Church. We exhorted them and prayed with them, and I spoke in tongues. Some pronounced it genuine and from the Lord, and others pronounced it of the devil.

"We proceeded to Kirtland and stopped at John P. Greene's [his brother-in-law] who had just arrived there with his family. We rested a few minutes, took some refreshment, and started to see the Prophet. We went to his father's house and learned that he was in the woods, chopping. We immediately repaired to the woods, where we found the Prophet and two or three of his brothers chopping and hauling wood. Here my joy was full at the privilege of shaking the hand of the Prophet of God, and I received the sure testimony, by the Spirit of Prophecy, that he was all that any could believe him to be, a true Prophet. He was happy to see us, and bade us welcome. We soon returned to his house, he accompanying us.

"In the evening a few of the brethen came in, and we conversed together upon the things of the kingdom. He called upon me to pray; in my prayer I spoke in tongues. As soon as we arose from our knees the brethen flocked around him, and asked his opinion concerning the gift of tongues, that was upon me. He told them it was the pure Adamic language. Some said to him they expected he would condemn the gift Brother Brigham had, but he said, 'No, it is of God, and the time will come when Brother Brigham Young will preside over this church.' The latter part of this conversation was in my absence.

"We returned home in October, and made preparations for leaving our friends and families. In company with my brother, Joseph, I started for Kingston, upper Canada, on foot, in the month of December, the most of the way was through snow and mud one to two feet deep."[5]

He was commissioned by the Prophet, in July 1833, to gather up converts from the western part of New York State and lead them to Kirtland, Ohio. In the fall of that same year he conducted a small company of

Saints to Kirtland. This indeed was the beginning of his subsequent pioneering movement of people in groups from place to place. He thus early demonstrated to the Prophet and to himself his gifts of organization and leadership. His life from then on was largely one of active up-building of the Church of Christ on earth. His conversion to the Gospel as a whole scheme of life was sincere and final.

He was moved to accept the counsel of the Elders who urged converts to gather around the young Prophet Joseph Smith, then located at Kirtland, so that a city and a united community might be built up which should be worthy of the title "Zion," a name which had already been given by revelation to the little group of Latter-day Saints. "Gather up to Zion!" was the cry heard by converts in all the surrounding county. Kirtland was to become a city where the visible symbols of homes, farms, forges, schools, meeting-houses and a temple would typify the companionship and close communion of the Latter-day Saints.

In the autumn of 1833 he and Brother Kimball removed their families to Kirtland so that they might be near the Prophet and assist more definitely in the building of the new Church. He worked at his trade as painter, glazier and carpenter, which work was greatly needed in the new communities of Kirtland and neighborhood.

A reward for his help to the Prophet came soon after his move to Kirtland, when he met a fine young woman from New England who was a new convert to the Church, Miss Mary Ann Angell. She was deeply religious, of a good Puritan family and had been a member of the Free Will Baptist Church. They became good friends and in time were married, on February 18, 1834. She mothered the two little girls of her new husband, became his wise counselor and loving companion and the mother of a large family of her own.

Brigham's joy in the Prophet's character and work knew no bounds. He never tired of proclaiming his adherence to the restored Gospel as well as his allegiance to the Prophet of the new dispensation. He gave to Joseph not only repeated declarations of his loyalty, but proved this loyalty on countless occasions of stress and throughout a long life of devotion to his memory. He spent his entire life in bringing to fruition the great truths taught by the Prophet. He declared: "Joseph Smith has laid the foundation of the kingdom of God in the last days; others will rear the superstructure. He laid the foundation of the great fabric, and we have commenced to build upon it. If we do right, there will be an eternal increase among this people in talent, strength of intellect, and earthly wealth, from this time, henceforth, and forever."[6] His labors continued and were increased because of his willingness and ability to accept responsibility.

Improvement was the watchword of Brigham's entire life. Wherever he was, he studied the scriptures, read history and such publications as were accessible, remembering always the fundamental thought expressed by the Lord through the Prophet Joseph Smith, that "The glory of God is intelligence." (D. & C. 93:36.)

In the winter of 1835-36, in addition to his other labors, he attended the Hebrew School at Kirtland, taught by Prof. Joshua Seixas. This school was founded by revelation to the Prophet for the study of languages, grammar, philosophy, and kindred subjects, and was attended by all the leading Elders and men of the Church. It is probably one of the very first attempts in the United States of formal adult education. He relates in his Journal: "I remained at home in Kirtland during the fall and winter, occasionally going out and preaching to the neighboring branches. In the course of the winter there was a Hebrew school started, which I attended until February 22, 1836, when I was called upon by the Prophet to superintend the painting and finishing of the Temple, upon which I labored until March 27, when the Temple was so far finished as to be dedicated to the Lord by the Prophet, with the assembled Quorums of the Church and as many members as could possibly be accomodated. On this occasion the power of God was displayed, as recorded in the history of Joseph Smith."

He thus proved by his life that in order to become actually converted to the Truth one must remain active in its defense.

CHAPTER 4

THE FIGHT FOR RIGHT

IT IS a queer commentary on human nature that whenever great truth has been sent upon earth it has met with intense opposition from the great majority of people. The Gospel as preached by Christ himself and as restored by a modern prophet, Joseph Smith, is no exception to this rule. From the very inception of its restoration to the present time it has received ridicule and often abuse from those who refuse to investigate its claims or to analyze its teachings. Even those born in the church who should be its chief defenders, may through overweening ambition or sin, be caught by the sophistries of men to denounce their birthright. The probable reason for human aversion to truth is that the power of darkness seems to stalk in Truth's wake to confound its purpose and to nullify its power, if possible. Indeed before Joseph's first heavenly manifestation the power of evil was so mighty that he felt his own destruction was near. The most unfortunate phase of this fact is that this same dark power often overcomes those who have accepted truth and are within the fold, and should therefore be the defenders of the Light.

The Prophet was constantly persecuted for the truths he proclaimed. Soon after the organization of the Church such difficulties arose that he was forced to change his residence from town to town, and finally early in 1831 he moved from the State of New York into Kirtland, Ohio, "because of the enemy and for your sakes." Even while vigorous up-building was in progress, yet there were those within and without the Church who sought his destruction. Indeed Joseph Smith was persecuted from the time of his first confession of his glorious experience to his friend (?), the minister, until he suffered a martyr's death at the hands of a ruthless mob. It is necessary to remember these early experiences of the Church in order to understand the events which followed. This persecution was so terrible that it was well-nigh impossible for him to accomplish the great labor that lay before him.

After the establishment of Kirtland, which became the headquarters of the new and struggling Church, lands were purchased and divided, home sites assigned, and an attempt was here made to "share all things in common," or to establish again on earth the United Order or the Order of Enoch, as it was called. But persecution followed the people and leaders in Ohio as in New York State.

The spirit of missionary work was active amongst leaders and members of the Church from its earliest days. Many missionaries had been sent to Missouri which was then the western frontier of the United States. The people living on these fringes of civilization were a mixed lot of home-seekers and adventurers with all kinds of customs and beliefs, "Universalists, Atheists, Presbyterians, Methodists, Baptists and other professing Christians, priests and people,"[1] mixed with renegades from the East, lawless and vile outcasts, who had been forced to flee to the West for safety. Yet is was a new country with many possibilities.

Hence the West beckoned to the new converts of the Church and many venturesome spirits listened to its call and brought their "families and their all" to settle in the land which had been revealed to the Prophet as the place where the "Center Stake of Zion" was to be built. Also, the move of many members of the Church to Missouri was the result of the bitter persecution of enemies without the Church and of apostates within the fold, back in their homes in New York State and Ohio.

The call to Missouri came to the people as a possible escape from their enemies in Ohio. It was made at the first Kirtland Conference in June, 1831, and Jackson County, Missouri, was at that time designated as the possible "Zion" for the persecuted Saints. A group of people from Colesville, who had settled for a brief period in Thompson, near Kirtland, journeyed on to Missouri in midsummer of that year. Others quickly followed and in time there were sizeable branches of the Church in Missouri as well as in Ohio.

Naturally, the restless, roving, adventure - loving Missourians did not welcome the incoming, industrious Mormons who were buying lands and preparing to settle permanently. So trouble began to brew. Also the Mormons were constitutionally anti-slavery while most of the people were slave holders either by practice or by belief. With this renegade population of outlaws and adventurers the industrious, law-abiding, anti-slaveholding Mormons soon became vastly unpopular. Misunderstanding and persecution broke out here as elsewhere. It seemed at times that "all the devils from the infernal pit were united and foaming out their hate against the elders of the Church."[2] "How natural it was," wrote the Prophet, "to observe the degredation, leanness of intellect, ferocity and jealousy of a people that were nearly a century behind the times."[3] In desperation the people sent to their leaders in Ohio a plea for succor and relief from the terrible persecution to which they were subjected.

Thus was organized the famous Zion's Camp, whose purpose was to give aid to those who were being unjustly treated in Missouri. A call for volunteers went out among the people, and in May, 1834 they left Kirtland and at New Portage were organized into companies for the journey. The march was difficult; cholera broke out amongst the members with many deaths, and there was great dissatisfaction because its mission seemed unfulfilled. Yet it was a great testing time for all who undertook it. From the faithful, willing men of that Camp, the Quorums of the Twelve Apostles and Seventy were later selected. Brigham Young and his brother Joseph were of these groups.

Brigham says: "While the Prophet Joseph was gathering up the Elders of Israel to go up to Missouri and assist the brethren that had been driven from Jackson County, I was preaching and laboring for the support of my family. My brother Joseph Young arrived, and I requested him to go with me to Missouri. He hesitated; but while walking together a few days afterwards we met the Prophet, who said to him: 'Brother Joseph, I want you to go with us up to Missouri.' I informed the Prophet that my brother was doubtful as to his duty about going, to which the Prophet replied, 'Brother Brigham and Brother Joseph, if you will go with me in the camp to Missouri and keep my counsel, I promise you in the name of the Almighty, that I will lead you there and back again, and not a hair of your heads shall be harmed,' at which my brother Joseph presented his hand to the Prophet, as well as myself, to confirm the covenant. The brethren continued to come in from various parts of the country to Kirtland and on the 5th day of May we started for New Portage, the place appointed for organization."[4]

Brigham refers to some of the difficulties of these intrepid scouts whose faith was tried almost to the breaking point.

"In the fall of 1834, Denis Lake instituted a lawsuit before Justices Dowen and Hanson, against brother Joseph Smith, charging him $30 a month for going up in Zion's camp to Missouri, alleging that Joseph had promised him a lot of land. I was called up by the attorney for the prosecution, General Paine, and questioned. I was asked if I went up to Missouri with the said camp. I answered I did. I was asked what tools I took with me. I replied, a good gun and bayonet, plenty of ammunition, a dirk, an ax, a chisel, spade, hoe, and other necessary tools. I was asked what I meant to do with my gun and ammunition. I replied I meant to defend my property, myself and my brethren from thieves and robbers. I was asked how much I understood a lot of land to mean. I told them, in the burying yard it generally meant six feet. Joseph's attorney, Mr. Bissell, hearing me answer these and similar questions so readily and definitely, punched the prosecuting attorney on the shoulder and asked him if he had any more questions to ask that witness. He said no."[5] Thus again did Brigham meet the challenge and make good.

While in Kirtland the Church became firmly established. A temple to the Most High was completed and dédicated with great and glorious manifestations of the power of God. The First Presidency and the Quorum of the Twelve were organized and missionaries were sent out to the neighboring states, East and West and into Canada. The Quorum of Twelve Apostles was organized February 14, 1835. Brigham Young was the third one named as a member of that important Quorum. People were home-building and busy with their attempts to establish peaceful communities where righteousness could reign. The finances of the Church as of individuals were organized into storehouses, banks and other working concerns. A day of prosperity seemed to be dawning for the Church and its people.

Yet as time passed the struggle between Light and Darkness became more intense. The enemies of Light were ever on hand to criticize the Prophet of God and to impute to him unworthy motives. Indeed a number of the Apostles, those who were nearest to him and should have been his chief defenders, arose against him. His enemies declared he had favorites; he was no business-man; he had lost touch with God; and that he was everything vile and corrupt. The chief cause of complaint was the fact that he chose to follow the commandments of God rather than the counsel of ambitious men who sought position and preferment rather than the welfare of the Church.

Of these experiences Brigham says: "At this time the spirit of speculation, disaffection and apostasy imbibed by many of the Twelve, and which ran through all the Quorums of the Church, prevailed so extensively that it was difficult for any to see clearly the path to pursue."[6]

"Joseph, our Prophet, was hunted and driven, arrested and persecuted, and although no law was ever made in these United States that would bear against him, for he never broke a law, yet to my certain knowledge he was defendant in forty-seven lawsuits, and every time Mr. Priest was at the head of and led the band or mob who hunted and persecuted him. And when Joseph and Hyrum were slain in Carthage jail the mob, painted like Indians, was led by a preacher."[7]

"He passed through forty-seven lawsuits, and in the most of them I was with him. He was obliged to employ lawyers, and devise ways and means to shield himself from oppression. Lawyers would come to Joseph, professing to have been his friends, and palaver around him, to get a fee. I could see through them and read their evil intentions. He had to struggle through poverty and distress, being driven from pillar to post. I wondered many a time that he could endure what he did. The Lord gave him strength in all these afflications."[8]

An interesting incident which occurred at a later time is recalled by Brigham. "Joseph Smith was arraigned before Judge Austin A. King, on a charge of treason. The Judge inquired of Mr. Smith, 'Do you believe and teach the doctrine that in the course of time the Saints will possess the earth?' Joseph replied that he did. 'Do you believe that the Lord will raise up a kingdom that will fill the whole earth and rule over all other kingdoms, as the Prophet Daniel has said?' 'Yes, sir, I believe that Jesus Christ will reign king of nations as he does king of Saints.' 'Write that down, clerk; we want to fasten upon him the charge of treason, for if he believes this, he must believe that the State of Missouri will crumble and fall to rise no more.' Lawyer Doniphan said to the Judge, 'damn it, Judge, you had better make the Bible treason and have done with it.' "[9]

The reason for this unrelenting persecution may cause one to wonder. It is rather easy to understand why those who loved evil should be against the Prophet for as Brigham once said, "They hated him because he would not fellowship their wickedness."

But why should those who had received a certain testimony of the Truth — who with Joseph, according to their own undying testimonies, had actually seen an angel and heard his voice—ever deny that Joseph was a Prophet of God? That is a question that very much concerns us today. How can the leaders of the Church, who are righteous men, be so severely criticized by those who should be their staunch defenders?

The answer is not far to seek. Those who then or now place the welfare of the Church above their own personal ambition and who are living in harmony with all the requirements of the Gospel of Christ, never feel it in their hearts to criticize their leaders, from the President of the Church down to the Bishop or the least officer in the ward. That is certain. Those who leave the Church (in Joseph's day or today) advertise to the world that they are out of harmony with Church requirements in private practice, or are possessed of an overweening ambition for position or power, or have committed some sin that has darkened their perception of right and wrong. There can be no other answer to the query. If the leaders are unfit, their own misdeeds will eventually cause their apostasy or the power of God will remove them from office.

So reasoned Brigham Young when all the forces of earth and hell seemed arrayed against the harrassed Prophet, and so he stood his ground irrevocably as the Prophet's staunch defender.

A definite warning to critics was sounded by Brigham Young on one occasion. In speaking of Joseph's accusers he said: "I rose up, and in a plain and forcible manner told them that Joseph was a Prophet, and I knew it, and that they might rail and slander him as much as they pleased, they could not destroy the appointment of the Prophet of God, they could only destroy their own authority, cut the thread that bound them to the Prophet and to God, and sink themselves to hell."

Has not that fate been realized by most of those who became the Prophet's severe critics and accusers?

Their names are all but "blotted out" of time's book of remembrance, while Joseph's name is being more and more honored throughout the earth.

CHAPTER 5

AN EARLY CHURCH CRISIS

WHEN things go wrong with the people or when they refuse to take the counsel of the leaders and evil days come upon them, is it not the easiest and most usual thing for them to blame someone else, especially the Church leaders, for their dilemma? Sometimes we are inclined to think that there never was a time when the Church or the people were called upon to meet quite such difficult times as those through which we have been and are passing today. The pages of early Church history may tell us whether or not this is true.

Let us review briefly the events of that day. As noted, the city of Kirtland grew and the people prospered in spite of persecution in Ohio and in Missouri. The Kirtland Temple was dedicated in 1836 with a most glorious dedicatory service which lasted many days.[1] For a time thereafter everything seemed most favorable for the growth of the Church and the prosperity of the people. The memory of the great and marvelous heavenly manifestations of the early temple services seemed to rouse the people to renewed and more vigorous religious activity. The "School of the Prophets" was being held in the Temple; in fact its halls were quite generally filled day and night by different Priesthood quorums and other activities.

People began to flock into Kirtland and land was purchased, on credit mostly, and in brief a general feeling of unprecedented prosperity seemed to be "in the air." Mercantile establishments and other industrial plants expanded greatly their stock, on credit of course, looking to the growth of the city to make good their investments. In fact the conditions may be said to resemble the various "booms" which have been experienced throughout the country since that time. It is interesting to note that these conditions were not confined to Kirtland but were quite general throughout the United States at that time.

The Kirtland Safety Society Bank was founded during this period—in November, 1836—for the purpose of helping to finance the many undertakings of the Saints. It was founded with the highest motives and was officered by some of the leading brethren of the Church including the Prophet. Unfortunately, through prejudice, they were unable to obtain a state charter, but its purpose was so superior that it was felt to be as safe as the Church, and began its business operations.

Prosperity proved fatal to righteousness then as it has done before and since. As is often the case, people began to feel so secure in their own "power of purse" that they had little need of their Heavenly Father's guidance. Then, as so often happens, people began to borrow recklessly and to live extravagantly. The oft-repeated warnings of the Prophet to "keep out of debt," to "live within your means," fell on deaf ears and the people tired of the warning. Meanwhile many of those who flocked to Kirtland were so poor that they had to accept charity and consequently could not pay for their lands.

The cashier of the Kirtland Safety Bank, a man trusted by the Prophet and near to him in much of his business, fell into evil practices of the day and finally into actual sin. Others of the leaders were implicated and resented the Prophet's insistence on strict and honest business dealings, until finally the Prophet withdrew, for he could not countenance improper business methods.

Then came the crash or the financial panic of 1837! This was a national crisis and is most interesting to review because its cause and the effects resulting therefrom are similar in many ways to the financial panic of nearly one hundred years later.

We read: "In order that it may be seen—after frankly admitting the folly and sin of the saints in these matters—that the financial failures of the Saints at Kirtland were not purely local, nor due to any principle connected with Mormonism, but were part of a general financial and industrial maelstrom that swept through the country, I quote the following from Alexander H. Stephens' History of the United States:

" 'Soon after Mr. Van Buren became president occurred a great commercial crisis. This was in April, 1837, and was occasioned by a reckless spirit of speculation, which had, for two or three preceding years, been fostered and encouraged by excessive banking, and the consequent expansion of paper currency beyond all the legitimate wants of the country. During the months of March and April of this year the failures in New York City alone amounted to over $100,000,000.'

"Another authority says: 'The great extent of the business operations of the country at that time, and their intimate connection with each other, extended the evil throughout all the channels of trade; causing, in the first place, a general failure of the mercantile interests—affecting, through them, the business of the mechanic and the farmer, nor stopping until it had reduced the wages of the humblest day laborer.' "[2]

How familiar this sounds to our ears and how similar to conditions in 1931! Naturally, as a result of these conditions, and when the State failed to recognize the notes of the Safety Bank, the complete collapse of that and other institutions and industries was inevitable. Then people rushed to place the blame on the Prophet and to accuse him of all possible crimes as though he alone were responsible for their financial undoing.

The effect of these events on the Church at this time was almost tragic. Many of the leading brethen, who had stood nearest to the Prophet from the restoration of the Church, became disaffected and through allowing ambition or greed to enter their hearts became subject to the powers of darkness. Satan seemed to be turned loose in their midst until the very air was foul with threats of apostasy and accusation of those who were righteous, lived simply, and kept themselves pure in heart.

The Prophet's courage was admirable. He could not temporize with evil, even though it might come from a member of his dear and loved ones or from his nearest friends, by whose side he had stood in the presence of angels.

It is remarkable and astonishing, too, that among Joseph's most active accusers were many of the witnesses to the Book of Mormon, and indeed his "right hand men" in the building up of the Church. Had he not been truly a man of God and a true Prophet, with an unquestioning certainty of his own calling, he would not have dared to call these men to account or to excommunicate them for their misbehavior. Yet he was fearless when it was a question of right and wrong. During all these months, as indeed throughout his entire lifetime, Brigham Young stood by the side and in defense of the Prophet for he knew that his leader was, above everything else, an honest man whom God had chosen to re-establish the restored Gospel of Christ on earth. Brigham says of him in this respect: "Joseph Smith was a rod in the hands of the Lord to scourge the Elders of Israel; he was the mouthpiece of the Almighty, and was always ready to rebuke them when requisite. You who were acquainted with him know his course and life. He had a word of comfort and consolation to the humble and faithful, and a word of rebuke to the forward and disobedient."[3]

Brigham recalls these incidents at a later date, in Salt Lake City: "Our situation is peculiar at the present time. Has it not been peculiar ever since Joseph found the plates? The circumstances that surrounded him when he found the plates were singular and strange. He passed a short life of sorrow and trouble, surrounded by enemies who sought day and night to destroy him. If a thousand hounds were on this Temple Block, let loose on one rabbit, it would not be a bad illustration of the situation at times of the Prophet Joseph. He was hunted unremittingly."[4]

"I have known persons that would have cursed brother Joseph to the lowest hell hundreds of times, because he would not trust out everything he had on the face of the earth, and let the people squander it to the four winds. When he had let many of the brethren and sisters have goods on trust, he could not meet his liabilities, and then they would turn round and say, 'What is the matter, brother Joseph, why don't you pay your debts?' 'It is quite a curiosity that you don't pay your debts; you must be a bad financier; you don't know how to handle the things of this world.' At the same time the coats, pants, dresses, boots and shoes that they and their families were wearing came out of Joseph's store, and were not paid for when they were cursing him for not paying his debts."[5]

Some amusing incidents occurred about this time, as Brigham relates it, showing how they had to use their wits to escape their tormentors: "A man named Howley, while plowing his field in the State of New York, had an impression rest down on his mind, with great weight, that he must go to Kirtland and tell Joseph Smith that the Lord had rejected him as a Prophet. He accordingly started right off, with his bare feet, and, on arriving in Kirtland, told Joseph that the Lord had rejected him for allowing John Noah, a Prophet of God, to be cut off from the Church and for allowing the women to wear caps and the men to wear cushions on their best coat sleeves. He was called up before the Bishop's court and disfellowshipped.

"He went through the streets of Kirtland one morning, after midnight, and cried, 'Woe! woe! unto the inhabitants of this place.' I put my pants and shoes on, took my cow-hide, went out, and laying hold of him, jerked him around, and assured him that if he did not stop his noise, and let the people enjoy their sleep without interruption, I would cow-hide him on the spot, for we had the Lord's Prophet right here, and we did not want the Devil's prophet yelling round the streets. The nuisance was forwith abated."[6]

It may be noted that the man referred to in the incident just quoted was well named!

The absolute defense of the Prophet and the loyalty of Brigham Young during these trying times was unquestioned. Let us not suppose, however, that Brigham was alone in this defense. All those who were pure in heart, who loved and lived righteousness had a certain testimony of the Prophet's honor. Amongst them and in addition to Brigham Young were Heber C. Kimball, Wilford Woodruff, John Taylor, Willard Richards, and other stalwart defenders of Truth. But in the vigorous defense of the Prophet, Brigham took the lead and defied heaven and hell and leaders or members of the Church to say aught against the man whom he knew to be a true Prophet of God.

One writer has said of this experience: "The strength of Brigham Young's character broke the tide of apostasy arising among the very leaders of the Church. There were in it no less than four of the Twelve Apostles, several of the 'witnesses of the Book of Mormon,' and many influential elders. To this day it has been a wonder among 'gentile' writers that the Prophet dared to excommunicate so many of his first elders at one grand sweep. It means that Joseph and Brigham, 'with the Lord on their side,' were equal to anything. The part that Brigham Young acted then made him the successor of Joseph Smith."[7]

Brigham's constant defense of the Prophet as he describes events which took place is wise and pointed. "Who can justly say aught against Joseph Smith? I was as well acquainted with him as any man. I do not believe that his father and mother knew him any better than I did. I do not think that a man lives on the earth that knew him any better than I did; and I am bold to say that, Jesus Christ excepted, no better man ever lived or does live upon this earth. I am his witness. He was persecuted for the same reason that any other righteous person has been or is persecuted at the present day."[8]

"On a certain occasion several of the Twelve, the witnesses to the Book of Mormon, and others of the Authorities of the Church, held a council in the upper room of the Temple. The question before them was to ascertain how the Prophet Joseph could be deposed, and David Whitmer appointed President of the Church. Father John Smith, brother Heber C. Kimball and others

were present, who were opposed to such measures. * * *
Many were highly enraged at my decided opposition
to their measures, and Jacob Bump (an old pugilist)
was so exasperated that he could not be still. Some of
the brethren near him put their hands on him, and requested him to be quiet; but he writhed and twisted
his arms and body saying, 'How can I keep my hands
off that man?' I told him if he thought it would give
him any relief he might lay them on. This meeting was
broken up without the apostates being able to unite on
any decided measures of opposition. This was a crisis
when earth and hell seemed leagued to overthrow the
Prophet and Church of God. The knees of many of the
strongest men in the Church faltered.

"During this siege of darkness I stood close by
Joseph, and, with all the wisdom and power God bestowed upon me, put forth my utmost energies to sustain the servant of God and unite the Quorums of the
Church."[9]

CHAPTER 6

A LEADER AMIDST MOB VIOLENCE

B RIGHAM YOUNG'S firm stand during the great crises in the rise of the Church, discussed in preceding chapters, added greatly to the comfort of the Prophet and gave courage to the family and other loyal friends of the troubled leader.

There was a definite reaction against Brigham, naturally, because of his opposition to the Prophet's enemies. They quickly turned their wrath against him and accused him of being in league with Joseph for selfish motives.

In his autobiography Brigham says of this turn of events: "On the morning of December 22, 1837, I left Kirtland in consequence of the fury of the mob and the spirit that prevailed in the apostates, who had threatened to destroy me because I would proclaim, publicly and privately, that I knew, by the power of the Holy Ghost, that Joseph Smith was a Prophet of the most high God, and had not transgressed and fallen as apostates declared."

The Prophet, too, continued to be persecuted. There seemd no safety for him anywhere. Hounded, while tarrying at Hiram, Portage County, Ohio, he was dragged out of the house by a mob, who tore him out of his wife's arms, carried him into an adjoining meadow, tarred and feathered him, and put aquafortis in his mouth. Sidney Rigdon was treated with the same indignities. The Prophet, however, undaunted by this brutal treatment preached next day with his flesh all scarified and defaced, proving the folly of persecution by baptizing three new converts at the close of the services.

In the year 1837, Brigham decided to leave his newly built home and all his earthly possessions in Kirtland, Ohio, and with his family move into the new

frontier and help build up the "Center Stake." After
he had set out, the Prophet also decided to journey westward. He joined Brigham at Dublin, Indiana, where he
attempted to find work that he might get means sufficient to proceed on his journey.

Brigham tells of one interesting incident on that
journey: "One day while crossing a large prairie, six or
eight miles from any house, we crossed a small stream.
The ground was frozen deep on each side, and we sprung
one of the axletrees of brother Barnard's carriage. Brother
Barnard said we could not travel with it any further.
Brother Joseph looked at it and said, 'I can spring that
axletree back, so that we can go on our journey.' Brother
Barnard replied: 'I am a blacksmith, and used to work
in all kinds of iron, and that axletree is bent so far
round that to undertake to straighten it would
only break it.' Brother Joseph answered, 'I'll try it.'
He got a pry, and we sprung it back to its place, and it
did not trouble us any more till we arrived at Far West.
Brother Barnard, seeing this done, concluded that he
would never say again that a thing could not be done
when a Prophet said it could."[1]

In Missouri, things seemed to go from bad to worse.
It is difficult to comprehend the cruelty of the Missourians toward the stricken "Mormon" refugees who sought
only to till the soil, live in peace according to law, and
worship God as they saw fit.

Mob spirit was aroused and the people instigated a
fierce crusade against the "Mormons," culminating in
the so-called exterminating order of Governor Boggs.
Generals Lucas and Clark were empowered to drive the
"Mormons en masse" and by any means, out of the
State of Missouri. Their cruelty is almost unbelievable.
We are told that "many of the Mormons were wounded

and murdered and several women were ravaged to death."
Of these events Brigham relates the following: "As soon
as the Missourians had laid by their corn as they called
it, they commenced to stir up the old mob spirit, riding
from neighborhood to neighborhood making inflamma-
tory speeches, stirring up one another against us. Priests
seemed to take the lead in this matter, as related in
the history. I had no communication, correspondence or
deal with the Missourians, consequently they did not
personally know me, which gave me a good opportunity
to learn their acts and feelings unsuspected. I knew men
in the course of the Fall to gather up their flocks and
herds and take their families into their wagons, and then
burn up their houses and leave for other parts. I afterwards saw their names attached to affidavits, stating
that Mormons had driven them from their homes and
burned their houses. This was quite effectual in raising
prejudice against us."[2]

"I saw Brothers Joseph Smith, Sidney Rigdon, Parley
P. Pratt, Lyman Wight and George W. Robinson delivered up by Colonel Hinkle to General Lucas, but expected
they would have returned to the city that evening or the
next morning, according to agreement, and the pledge
of the sacred honor of the officers that they should be
allowed to do so, but they did not so return. The next
morning Gen. Lucas demanded and took away the arms
of the militia of Caldwell County, assuring the people
that they should be protected; but as soon as they obtained possession of their arms, they commenced their
ravages by plundering the citizens of their bedding, clothing, money, wearing apparel, and every thing of value
they could lay their hands upon, and also attempted to
violate the chastity of the women in the presence of
their husbands and friends. The soldiers shot down our

oxen, cows, hogs and fowls at our own doors, taking part
away and leaving the rest to rot in the streets. They also
turned their horses into our fields of corn."[3]

So much animosity was aroused that finally the
Governor of the state, Lilburn W. Boggs, issued a declara-
tion that the Mormons must leave the state or take the
consequences. "You need not expect any mercy, but
extermination," said General Clark as he delivered the
Governor's order. "As for your leaders, do not think,
do not imagine for a moment, do not let it enter into
your minds that they will be delivered and restored to
you again, for their fate is fixed, the die is cast, their
doom is sealed."[4]

" ' I was present,' says Brigham, 'when that speech
was delivered, and when fifty-seven of our brethren were
betrayed into the hands of our enemies as prisoners.
General Clark said that we must not be seen as
many as five together; "if you are," said he, "the citizens
will be upon you and destroy you; but you should flee
immediately out of the State. There is no alternative for
you but to flee; you need not expect any redress; there
is none for you." '

"With respect to the treaty mentioned by Gen.
Clark, I have to say that there never was any treaty
proposed or entered into on the part of the Mormons, or
any one called a Mormon, except by Col. Hinkle. And
with respect to the trial of Joseph and the brethren at
Richmond, I did not consider that tribunal a legal court
but an inquisition. The brethren were compelled to give
away their property at the point of the bayonet."[5]

A vivid account of the atrocities committed against
the Saints is given by Hyrum Smith: "The same men
sat as a jury in the day time, and were placed over us
as a guard in the night time. They tantalized and boasted

over us, of their great achievements at Haun's Mill and at other places, telling us how many houses they had burned, and how many sheep, cattle, and hogs they had driven off belonging to the Mormons, and how many rapes they had committed. * * * These fiends of the lower regions boasted of these acts of barbarity, and tantalized our feelings with them for ten days. We had heard of these acts of cruelty previous to this time, but we were slow to believe that such acts of cruelty had been perpetrated.

"This grand jury constantly celebrated their achievements with grog and glass in hand, like the Indian warriors at their war dances, singing and telling each other of their exploits in murdering the 'Mormons,' in plundering their houses and carrying off their property. At the end of every song they would bring in the chorus, 'God damn God, God damn Jesus Christ, God damn the Presbyterians, God damn the Baptists, God damn the Methodists,' reiterating one sect after another in the same manner, until they came to the Mormons. To them it was, 'God damn the God-damned Mormons, we have sent them to hell.' Then they would slap their hands and shout, Hosanna! Hosanna! Glory to God! and fall down on their backs and kick with their feet a few moments. Then they would pretend to have swooned away into a glorious trance, in order to imitate some of the transactions, at camp meetings. Then they would pretend to come out of the trance, and would shout and again slap their hands and jump up, while one would take a bottle of whiskey and a tumbler, and turn it out full of whiskey, and pour down each other's necks, crying, 'Damn it, take it; you must take it.' And if any one refused to drink the whiskey, others would clinch him and hold him, whilst another poured it down his

neck; and what did not go down the inside went down
the outside. This is a part of the farce acted out by
the grand jury of Daviess County, whilst they stood
over us as guards for ten nights successively. And all
this in the presence of the great Judge Birch, who had
previously said, in our hearing, that there was no law
for the Mormons in the State of Missouri.".[6]

Can anyone wonder why the Mormon people in their
later history dreaded and feared anyone who claimed
to be from Missouri? Is it not rather to be wondered at
that, being human, they enacted so few deeds of cruelty
and revenge for the most inhuman treatment which they
suffered again and again? Certainly there are far fewer
cruelties charged against the Mormons than against the
settlers of any of the western frontier territories.

Brigham Young became an emergency leader. After
the arrest of Joseph and so many of the leading brethren,
Brigham Young and the few leaders who were free were
asked to assume control of the affairs of the stricken
Saints. When the Quorum of Apostles was organized,
Brigham was third on the list. Thomas B. Marsh, the
first of the Quorum, deserted the Church in a fit of
anger in October, 1838, and was excommunicated for
apostasy in March, 1839. David W. Patten, the second
of the Quorum, was shot at the Battle of Crooked River
in October, 1838, thus leaving Brigham Young the
senior or leader of the Quorum of the Twelve.

The Prophet and his brethren in jail were treated
with untold cruelty, yet he continued to send out instructions whenever possible. However, it became im-
perative that the people should be removed from Missouri or be literally exterminated from the face of the
earth. In this crisis Brigham again became "the man
of the hour," and called the most active of the remain-

ing brethren together and made the necessary plans for their removal from Missouri into the State of Illinois, which State gave them a temporary but a most appreciated welcome.

"A leader in distress," Brigham might have been called at that time. He says: "In February, 1839, I left Missouri with my family, leaving my landed property and also my household goods, and went to Illinois, to a little town called Atlas, Pike County, where I tarried a few weeks; then moved to Quincy.

"I held a meeting with the brethren of the Twelve and the members of the Church in Quincy, on the 17th of March, when a letter was read to the people from the committee, on behalf of the Saints at Far West, who were left destitute of the means to move. Though the brethren were poor and stripped of almost everything, yet they manifested a spirit of willingness to do their utmost, offering to sell their hats, coats and shoes to accomplish the object. We broke bread and partook of the sacrament. At the close of the meeting $50 was collected in money, and several teams were subscribed to go and bring the brethren. Among the subscribers was the widow of Warren Smith, whose husband and two sons had their brains blown out at the massacre at Haun's Mill. She sent her only team on this charitable mission."[7]

Brigham's tender sympathy and exceeding care in detail of execution were taxed to the utmost; but the bereaved widows and the fatherless children were especially remembered and all carefully transported to safety. He required all the leading men in his company to covenant that they would never rest until the poor with every helpless woman and child were removed safely and comfortably to their new dwelling place. He left his own family eleven times to assist the more helpless ones to get away from the mobs of Missouri.

His journal at this time records these facts: "We entered into a covenant to see the poor Saints all moved out of Missouri to Illinois, that they might be delivered out of the hands of such vile persecutors, and we spared no pains to accomplish this object until the Lord gave us the desires of our hearts. We had the last company of the poor with us that could be removed. Brothers P. P. Pratt and Morris Phelps were in prison, and we had to leave them for a season. We sent a wagon after Brother Yokum, who had been so dreadfully mutilated in the Haun's Mill massacre that he could not be moved.

"We started early this morning from the Grove; the company consisted of seven of the Twelve, several of the committee left at Far West to close up business, and a few families of the Saints. We continued our journey to the Mississippi River, and on the 2nd of May we crossed on the steam ferry-boat to Quincy, Illinois."[8]

Thus Brigham secured of necessity a training in the leadership and removal of large numbers of people, which was to prove so useful to him in his later life. He was being drilled in the hard school of necessity for future and greater service.

The story of the escape of the Prophet Joseph and other leading brethren from their unjust imprisonment in foul jails in Missouri is well-known to students of Church history. Also the purchase of a small townsite on the banks of the Mississippi River called "Commerce" and of its transformation from a plague spot to a place of rural beauty is equally well-known. The water-soaked land was drained, and through sheer persistence and industry a thriving city gradually was built and named Nauvoo (called The Beautiful). It soon became the largest city in Illinois; Chicago was then but a trading post. Here the driven people worked and throve and hoped to live in peace.

CHAPTER 7

A CALL TO THE MISSION FIELD

THE Gospel of Jesus Christ was restored for the benefit of every one of God's earth children. Therefore, one scarcely need ask: Does this Gospel belong to the world—to every son of Adam? Or is this an American church for the few members primarily and the missions incidentally?

The missionary spirit is a part of one's testimony of the truth of the restored and complete Gospel of Jesus Christ. No one has ever received this testimony without wanting to "tell the world" all about it—as many as will listen—that others too may share the joy possessed by the true convert. In that sense, every bona fide member of this Church is a potential missionary from the time of his conversion. Indeed, his sincerity may often be tested by just that very measuring rod. Certainly this was true of Brigham Young.

In considering his activity on behalf of the spread of truth on earth, we shall have to retrace our steps somewhat according to the chronology of the events of his life, for his career as an active missionary began soon after he joined the Church.

His inward call to active missionary service may be said to date from the hour of his baptism, or before. Never did he lose an opportunity to bear his testimony of the fulness of the restored Gospel and the divinity of the mission of the Prophet Joseph.

He later tells of these early experiences and explains how incapable he felt himself to be: "Often, when I stand up here, I have the feelings of a person that is unable to convey his ideas, because I have not the advantage of language. However, I do not very fre-

quently complain of that, but I rise to do the best I
can and to give the people the best I have for them at
the time. How I have had the headache, when I had
ideas to lay before the people, and not words to express them; but I was so gritty that I always tried my
best. When I think of myself, I think just this—I have
the grit in me, and I will do my duty anyhow. When
I began to speak in public, I was about as destitute of
language as a man could well be."[1]

"In my early career as a preacher of the Gospel I
was ignorant of letters to a great degree, yet I have
been a Bible student from my youth; but when the
Spirit of the Lord was upon me it was no matter to
me who heard my voice when declaring the principles
of the Gospel, or who felt disposed to dispute, criticise,
or spiritualize or do away with the Scriptures of divine
truth. To me it was nothing; they were like children,
and their efforts were no more than the efforts of babes."[2]

"When I used to be preaching in the world, priests
would come to me and inquire about my doctrine. I
would tell them my principles—every principle that I
could get plainly before them would be for their
good; and after giving them my doctrine, I would ask,
What do you Methodists believe? They would tell me
. . . . I understood the whole concern, yet my religion
embraced all the truth they all had and a great deal
more. . . . I would say, I know how much truth you
have embraced; you have bounds to your religion, but
I have no bounds to mine; the faith I have embraced is
broad as eternity."[3]

His first definite missionary assignment came to him
from the Prophet when in May, 1835, he was sent with
some of the Twelve (which quorum had recently been
organized) to preach the Gospel to the Lamanites. In

making this call the Prophet said, "This will open the door to all the seed of Joseph." That entire summer was spent in this activity.

The next year, soon after the marvelous manifestations at the dedication of the Kirtland Temple, he was sent with his brother Joseph to the Eastern States, where they toured and preached in Vermont, Massachusetts, and New York State.

Some of his later experiences he afterwards described: "The second time I went to Canada, which was after I was baptized, myself and my brother Joseph traveled two hundred and fifty miles in snow a foot and a half deep, with a foot of mud under it. We traveled, preached, and baptized forty-five in the dead of winter. When we left there, the Saints gave us five York shillings with which to bear our expenses two hundred and fifty miles on foot, and one sister gave me a pair of woolen mittens, two-thirds worn out. I worked with my own hands and supported myself."[4]

"I used to take my carriage rides on foot, traveling and preaching from neighborhood to neighborhood, and from people to people, but we were not in the midst of the Saints. I told those brethren that I was well paid— paid with heavy interest—yea that my measure was filled to overflowing with the knowledge that I had received by traveling with the Prophet."[5]

His methods of preaching the already somewhat unpopular Gospel were unique and most effective. Were he practicing them today one would be apt to ascribe to him a very practical knowledge of the science of psychology, as evidenced by his wise application of its many truths. He says regarding this point: "The Lord has given me the ability that whenever I have wished to receive favors from those who knew me not I have ob-

tained them. I know it is the custom of many Elders
to say, 'I am a Mormon Elder; will you keep me over
night?' and he is at once spurned from the doors of
the stranger. Whether it is a credit to me or not, I
never told them I was a Mormon Elder until I got what
I wanted. I have thus stopped at many a house, and
had the privilege of introducing the principles of our
religion, and they have exclaimed, 'Well, if this is Mormonism, my house shall be your home as long as you
stay in this neighborhood,' when perhaps, if I had said,
'I am a Mormon Elder at the first they would have
refused me their hospitality.

"Thus, for me to travel and preach without purse
or script, was never hard; I never saw the day, I never
was in the place, nor went into a house, when I was
alone, or when I would take the lead and do the talking, but what I could get all I wanted. I would make the
acquaintance of the family, and sit and sing to them and
chat with them, and they would feel friendly towards
me; and when they learned that I was a Mormon Elder,
it was after I had gained their good feelings.

"I can say to the world they used me pretty well,
and I have no fault to find with them in this respect.
I have been abused sometimes by priests, but on such
occasions I have ever been ready to defend the cause
of righteousness and preach the gospel to all. The Elders
of Israel have received more kindness from the infidel
portions of mankind where they have traveled, than
from those who profess Christianity."[6]

"I will here say, however, that I have been treated
kindly when traveling among strangers to preach this
gospel. I do not know that I ever asked for a meal of
victuals without obtaining it. Still, I have seen enough
from the experience of others to know the real feel-

ings, and to understand the desires of the ungodly concerning the Elders of Israel. They do not desire them any good."

Another reason for his success in the ministry is hinted at in the following: "I have traveled a great deal in the world; and though, through the evil that is within me, it is natural for me to contend, and if I am opposed to oppose in return, and if a sharp word is spoken to me to give a sharp word back, I have done so but rarely. It is wrong, and we must subdue the inclination."[7]

"As I used to say to the ministers, when traveling and preaching, 'I will not dispute. If you want the truth I will give it to you; and if you have a truth that I have not, I want all you have; but contention is not my calling; it is no part of the Gospel of Christ; that is peace, life, light, and salvation. The Lord has given that to me and you, and you are welcome to it."[8]

How wise this view, and how blessed are the labors of the missionary who can remember and practice this wise psychological truth! Self-control is often the essence of excellence and success in any line of endeavor.

His wide vision of the Gospel is partly expressed by him thus: "How often, when I was engaged in traveling and preaching the Gospel, have the people said to me, 'O, this must be all a speculation! You differ so much from other people that we cannot believe all you teach.' 'We have heard a great deal about Mr. Smith,' or 'Joe Smith,' they would often say, 'and he must be a speculator, and these doctrines you preach were gotten up by him expressly for a speculation.' I have acknowledged a great many times, and I am as free to acknowledge it is today, that it is the greatest speculation ever entered into by God, men, or angels, for it is a speculation involving eternal lives in the celestial kingdom of God. It is the grandest investment on the face of the earth, and one in which you may invest all and everything you possess for the present and eternal benefit of yourself, your wives, your children, parents, relatives and friends; and all who are wise will enter into it, for they can make more of it, and be exalted higher by its means than by any other speculation ever introduced among the children of men. Happiness and glory are the pursuit of every person that lives on the face of the earth, who is thoroughly endowed with wisdom and the spirit of enterprise, whether immortality is brought in or not. Such are after honor, ease, comfort; such want to wield power, and would like to have influence and dominion. Now, if they will enter this great speculation—the kingdom of God on the earth, and plan of redemption and exaltation devised before the foundation of the world was laid—it will lead to greater happiness, power, influence, and dominion than ever man possessed or thought of."[9]

His practical outlook was expressed by him at another time: "I recollect a lady asking me in Canada, in 1832 or '33, how large Jackson County was; and when I said 30 miles square, said she, 'Suppose the whole world would embrace your doctrine, how would they get into Jackson County?' My reply was that, 'Jackson County,' in that case, would cover the whole world. Zion will expand as far as the necessity of the case requires it. You need not fear but there will be room for you, if you believe and gather with the Saints."[10]

Does this not definitely foreshadow the extension of the stakes of Zion as they exist and will exist in different parts of the world today?

His attitude to would-be persecutors and those who loved not righteousness was tersely expressed by him in his later life: "As I said when I commenced preaching twenty-three years ago and saw the same spirit of persecution exhibited then as subsequently, 'Let us alone, persecutors, we do not wish to fight you, for we have not come to destroy men's lives, or to take peace from the earth, but we have come to preach the Gospel, and to make known to you the things of the Kingdom of God. If your doctrine is better than ours, let us know it, for we are searching after the true riches, we wish the light of heaven to accompany us, we are searching after salvation, and if we have anything better than you have, you are welcome to it. But just let us alone, for we are determined, in the name of Israel's God, not to rest until we have revolutionized the world with truth; and if you persecute us, we will do it the quicker.'[11]

"As I have said before, I have often gone incog., and taught persons the Gospel, and they would drink down its principles as eargerly as a thirsty ox would drink water; but an ignorant prejudice causes all the trouble. The excitement among the priests, and directed by politicians, raises this erroneous prejudice and hue-and-cry."[12]

His financial outlay for his missionary labor was often referred to by him. One interesting item follows: "I have traveled and preached a great deal, and had to live, and I have always had a large family to support. I have had to borrow money to come home with, and I do not remember that I ever brought any money home, but what it has gone directly to relieve the Prophet of his burdens. He used to ask me how I managed to support myself and family. I told him that I made a six-pence go, perhaps, as far as some would make a quarter of a dollar go—that I had done what I could, and the Lord had done the rest, and that was all I knew about it."[13]

How typical of him that his beloved file-leader and friend should be the first to receive of any surplus he may have received for any labor. He was essentially a generous man. Yet there was often something almost miraculous in the way the money for missionary labor came to him.

What is a miracle? Sir Oliver Lodge in one of his books says: "Some may use the term **miracle** to mean the utilization of unknown laws—laws whereby time and space appear temporarily suspended." In other words, a miracle is an event occasioned by laws which may be perfectly natural but with which we may not be familiar. In that sense it certainly was miraculous the way Brigham was provided with means for his many labors.

"I do know that Heber C. Kimball and myself used $86.00 in board and other expenses when traveling on a mission, and that when we started we had but $13.50. And I do know that I once took a five-dollar bill out of my pocket, when we were raising money for brother Joseph and threw it in, and that the next day I had just as much as I had before I gave away the five dollars. I do know that when I went to pay some money that I owed, after giving some away to the poor, I had just as much when I came to pay my debts as I had before I gave any to the poor. I do know that I handed out a half-eagle in my pocket that I never put there. And I also do know that I never hungered or thirsted for property."[14]

The rigors of these early experiences are scarcely dreamed of by our missionaries today. For instance, after his active missionary experience he once said:

"When I returned from England, I said it is the last time I will travel as I have done, unless the Lord specially requires me to do so; for if we could ride even as comfortably as brother Woodruff once rode on one of the Mississippi steam boats, we considered ourselves well off. All the bed he had was the chines of barrels, with his feet hanging on a brace, and he thought himself well off to get the privilege of riding in any shape, to escape constant walking."[15]

Yet the rewards of this work were well-known to this stalwart missionary. "Brother Kimball referred to Zion's camp going to Missouri. When I returned from that mission to Kirtland, a brother said to me, 'Brother Brigham, what have you gained by this journey?' I replied, 'Just what we went for; but I would not exchange the knowledge I have received this season for the whole of Geauga County; for property and mines of wealth are not to be compared to the worth of knowledge.' Ask those brethren and sisters who have passed through scenes of affliction and suffering for years in this Church, what they would take in exchange for their experience, and be placed back where they were, were it possible. I presume they would tell you, that all the wealth, honors, and riches of the world could not buy the knowledge they had obtained, could they barter it away."[16]

"I know not what it is to go without food since I have been a Mormon. I could travel over the earth without purse or scrip, and not be obliged to go hungry. Before I knew Mormonism I was acquainted with straitened circumstances, but Mormonism has clothed and fed me, and blessed me all the day long."[17]

CHAPTER 8

BRIGHAM GOES ABROAD — HIS FOREIGN MISSIONS

T HE foreign missions of the Church were undertaken amidst deep trials and persecution of the Kirtland period. The Prophet was inspired to call some of the faithful brethren in the Church to spread abroad the message of restored Truth. The man chosen to lead this first mission was Heber C. Kimball, Brigham's dearest friend from youth. Indeed, Heber was so loath to go without Brigham that he plead with the Prophet that Brigham might be of the party. This was refused, for the Prophet felt that there was a greater work for Brigham to do at home; and so it proved. He became an active figure in the Prophet's defense, as we have learned from previous chapters.

On June 23, 1837, the first group of missionaries for England and other European countries set sail from New York. In this group from Kirtland went Heber C. Kimball, Orson Hyde, and Willard Richards (Brigham's cousin, a recent convert and a most devout and superior man); also four young men from Canada— Joseph Fielding, Isaac Russell, John Snyder, and John Goodson. They landed in Liverpool on July 20th and were the first to begin on European soil to accomplish literally a "marvelous work and a wonder." About a year later, some of these brethren returned to their homes, leaving Willard Richards in charge of the mission.

At home in Kirtland during this trouble-filled period, the Prophet received a revelation concerning the Twelve taking foreign missions "over the great waters," but it was not until 1839 that this materialized.

This mission of the Twelve included Brigham Young, Heber C. Kimball, John Taylor, Wilford Woodruff, Or-

son Hyde, Parley P. Pratt, Orson Pratt, and George
A. Smith; also John E. Page, Hiram Clark, Reuben Hedlock, and Theodore Turley, who set out from Nauvoo at
different times. They were hindered through illness and
other causes in reaching their destinations. John Taylor,
Wilford Woodruff, and Theodore Turley arrived in Liverpool in January, 1840. Brigham Young and Heber C.
Kimball left their homes in September, 1839, but were
greatly delayed en route. It was not until March, 1840,
that Brothers Young, Kimball, George A. Smith, Parley
and Orson Pratt, and Reuben Hedlock sailed from New
York on board a small sailing packet, the "Patrick Henry."

Some preliminary experiences of Brothers Kimball
and Young are related by the former: "September 14,
President Brigham Young left his home at Montrose to
start on the mission to England. He was so sick that
he was unable to go to the Mississippi, a distance of
thirty rods, without assistance. After he had crossed the
river he rode behind Israel Barlow on his horse to my
house, where he continued sick until the 18th. He left
his wife sick with a babe only three weeks old, and all
his other children were sick and unable to wait upon
each other. Not one soul of them was able to go to the
well for a pail of water, and they were without a second
suit to their backs, for the mob in Missouri had taken
nearly all he had. On the 17th, Sister Mary Ann Young
got a boy to carry her up in his wagon to my house, that
she might nurse and comfort Brother Brigham to the
hour of starting.

"September 18, Charles Hubbard sent his boy with
a wagon and a span of horses to my house; our trunks
were put into the wagon by some brethren; I went to
my bed and shook hands with my wife who was then

shaking with a chill, having two children lying sick by her side; I embraced her and my children, and bade them farewell. My only well child was little Heber P., and it was with difficulty he could carry a couple of quarts of water at a time, to assist in quenching their thirst.

"It was with difficulty we got into the wagon and started down the hill about ten rods; it appeared to me as though my very inmost parts would melt within me at leaving my family in such a condition, as it were, almost in the arms of death. I felt as though I could not endure it. I asked the teamster to stop, and said to Brother Brigham, 'This is pretty tough,. isn't it; let's rise up and give them a cheer.' We arose, and swinging our hats three times over our heads, shouted: 'Hurrah, hurrah for Israel.' Vilate, hearing the noise, arose from her bed and came to the door. She had a smile on her face. Vilate and Mary Ann Young cried out to us: 'Goodby, God bless you.' We returned the compliment, and then told the driver to go ahead. After this I felt a spirit of joy and gratitude, having had the satisfaction of seeing my wife standing upon her feet, instead of leaving her in bed, knowing well that I should not see them again for two or three years."[1]

All the other brethren had similiar experiences.

Brigham tells of his missionary labors as no other pen could do, and relates why they were delayed in taking their mission, also how they obtained the necessary finances for the trip. "I will relate an incident, which occurred during our journey to England. Brother George A. Smith accompanied me to New York City, and we had not enough to pay the last five miles' fare.

"We started from New Haven in a steam boat, and when we left the boat, I hired passage in the stage to

New York; the captain of the steam boat happened to be in the same stage.

"When we left the coach, I said to the captain, will you have kindness to pay this gentleman's passage and mine? I had had no conversation with him during the day, only in interchanging the common and usual compliments, but when we left him he greeted us cordially, and said that he had paid our stage-fare with the greatest pleasure, and shook our hands as heartily as a brother, saying, 'May God bless and prosper you in your labors.'

"It was not more than a week or ten days before we had been in fifty different places in New York City and the surrounding country, and those who came to hear us invited their neighbors, and thus we preached and baptized, and soon gathered means enough to defray the expenses of our passage to England, principally from those who were the fruits of our own labors."[2]

They arrived in England after an uneventful voyage and in the best of spirits. A description of the landing in England follows: "Liverpool was reached by these apostles on the 6th day of April. It was the anniversary of the organization of the church, just ten years before. Brigham left the ship in a boat, with Heber C. Kimball and Parley P. Pratt, and when he landed he gave a loud shout of Hosanna! They procurred a room at No. 8 Union Street, and here they partook of the sacrament, and returned thanks to God for his protecting care while on the waters, and prayed that their way might be opened to the successful accomplishment of their mission.

"Next day they found Elder Taylor and John Moon, with about thirty Saints who had just received the work in that place. On the following day they went to Preston by railroad (which was built just at the period that the Mormon mission was introduced to that country).

"In Preston, the cradle of the British mission, the apostles were met by a multitude of Saints, who rejoiced exceedingly at the great event of the arrival of the Twelve in that land."[3]

Brigham continues the story: "We went to Preston and held our Conference, and decided that we would publish a paper; brother Parley P. Pratt craved the privilege of editing it, and we granted him the privilege. We also decided to print three thousand hymn books, though we had not the first cent to begin with, and were strangers in a strange land. We appointed Brother Woodruff to Herefordshire, and I accompanied him on his journey to that place. I wrote to Brother Pratt for information about his plans, and he sent me his prospectus which stated that when he had a sufficient number of subscribers and money enough in hand to justify his publishing the paper, he would proceed with it. How long we might have waited for that I know not, but I wrote to him to publish two thousand papers, and I would foot the bill. I borrowed two hundred and fifty pounds [about $1250.00] of Sister Jane Benbow, one hundred [about $500.00] off Brother Thomas Kingston, and returned to Manchester, where we printed three thousand Hymn Books, and five thousand Books of Mormon, and issued two thousand 'Millennial Stars' monthly, and in the course of the summer printed and gave away rising of sixty thousand tracts. I also paid from five to ten dollars per week for my board, and hired a house for Brother Willard Richards and his wife who came to Manchester, and sustained them; and gave sixty pounds [about $300.00] to Brother P. P. Pratt to bring his wife from New York. I also commenced the emigration in that year.

"I was there one year and sixteen days, with my brethren the Twelve and during that time I bought all my clothing, except one pair of pantaloons, which the sisters gave me in Liverpool soon after I arrived there, and which I really needed. I told the brethren, in one of my discourses, that there was no need of their begging, for if they needed anything the sisters could understand that. The sisters took the hint, and the pantaloons were forthcoming.

"I paid three hundred and eighty dollars to get the work started in London, and when I arrived home, in Nauvoo, I owed no person one farthing. Brother Kington received his pay from the books that were printed, and Sister Benbow, who started to America the same year, left names enough of her friends to receive the two hundred and fifty pounds, which amount was paid them, notwithstanding I held her agreement that she had given it to the Church.

"We left two thousand five hundred dollars worth of books in the Office, paid our passages home, and paid about six hundred dollars for other purposes."[4]

"When I was in the old country I never was under the necessity of asking a penny from any person, and for which I have been thankful a thousand times since in reflecting upon it. I believe the only alms I ever asked, or the only intimation I ever gave of being in need, was on Long Island, when on my way to England. The brethren there, or rather those who were brethren afterwards, gave me some money. When I got to England, I had a few shillings left. While there the Lord put means into my hands, and after I was established in my office, I do not know that I ever went out without first putting into my pockets as many coppers as my hand could grasp, to give to the needy I met by the way, and I have fed and clothed many. I have been very thankful for this."⁵

It would be most interesting had we time to follow him in greater detail. He labored most assiduously, and with the cooperation of his associates organized the affairs of the Mission on such broad lines that the work grew and waxed strong under the hands of his successors.

A resume of his English missionary experiences follows: "When we went to England I was better off than many of my brethren, for I had enough to pay my expenses to Preston. On we went to that town, and held our Conference, and from thence we started out every way, preaching the Gospel in the regions round about.

"Allow me the privilege of boasting, though it is not me but the Lord that has done it. We sustained ourselves, and assisted the poor to a very large amount. This means was gathered up by faith, and we baptized over seven thousand people, gave away about sixty thousand tracts, for which I paid the money, and sent Elders out to preach in every direction."⁶

"I recollect when I left to go to England, I was unable to walk twenty rods without assistance. I was helped to the edge of the river Mississippi and carried across. When Brother Kimball and I started on our journey there was a struggle between us and the powers of earth and hell whether or not we should accomplish our mission. We were in the depths of poverty, caused by being driven from Missouri, where we had left all. I recollect that one of my own sisters pitied my condition and situation; she was sorry for me, and said, 'Brother Brigham, what necessity is there for you to go to England while you are sick? Why not tarry here until you are well?' I

said to her, as I started off one morning, 'Sister Fanny,
I never felt better in my life.' She was a very eccentric
woman and looking at me, with tears in her eyes, she
said, 'You lie.' I said nothing, but I was determined to
go to England or to die trying. My firm resolve was
that I would do what I was required to do in the Gospel
of life and salvation, or I would die trying to do it. I
am so today.

"We landed upon the shores of England, and then
I felt that the chains were broken, and the bands that
were upon me were burst asunder. . . . A few of the
Twelve and Seventies tarried in England. In these twelve
months and sixteen days, under my supervision, between
eight and nine thousand persons were baptized before
we left, branches of the Church were organized, the
emigration prepared, ships were chartered and companies
sailed out. . . . One of the finest vessels in the harbor
tied up eight days to carry myself and brethren across
the water. The agents of the vessel said such a thing
had never been done before, but they were urgent and
anxious to oblige us, for we had chartered and fitted out
several vessels, and as our emigration promised to be
a large business they wanted to carry us home. . . . Our
labor was successful, God blessed us, and when we returned, our Books of Mormon were paid for. The gentleman who bound the first Book of Mormon in England
binds them today when they have to be bound. We have
not owed the first farthing to those who have done this
work for us, but have paid promptly, according to promise, for every particle of our printing. Besides doing what
I have already mentioned in that twelve months, I sustained several families while there, and preserved them
from starvation and death. All this was through the
blessing of the Lord being upon us. We were strangers

and unknown in a strange land, but the work prospered under the hands of the Servants of God, and the means to do the work that was done, was procured through our industry and prudence. We organized the Church, we ordained two patriarchs, and from that time we have been gathering the poor."[7]

May not this be characterized as one of the greatest missionary accomplishments since the days of the Apostles of old? Brigham continues the narrative of missionary events: "When I landed in Liverpool I had six bits, and with that I bought me a hat. I had worn, on my journey to England, a little cap that my wife had made me out of a pair of pantaloons that I could not wear any longer. Did we beg? No. The brethren and sisters, and especially the sisters, would urge us to come and eat with them. I would try to beg off; but that would not do, it would hurt their feelings, we must go and eat their food, while they would starve to procure it. I was always ashamed of this; but I invariably had a sixpence to give them. How much had I given to me? One sister, who now lives in Payson, gave me a soverign [$5.00] and a pair of stockings; and when I came away a hatter, by the name of Miller, sent two hats by me to my little boys. . . . I might have received a shilling or two from others, but I do not recollect. When we left we sent over a shipload of the brethren and sisters, a good many of whose fares we paid.

"When I went into Liverpool I do not think I could have got trusted for a sixpence if I had gone into every store and shop in the place. When we came away a certain Captain wanted to bring us over, and said he, 'Are you ready?' 'No.' 'How long must I wait for you?' 'Eight days,' and they tied up one of the finest vessels in the harbor of Liverpool in order to bring us over.

I thought this was a miracle, don't you? I am sure there are some sisters now here who came with us in that vessel. I received that as a miracle. It was the hand of God. Was it our ability? No. Is it our ability that has accomplished what we see here in building up a colony in the wilderness? Is it the doings of man? No. To be sure we assist in it, and we do as we are directed. But God is our Captain; he is our master. He is the 'one man' that we serve. In him is our light, in him is our life; in him is our hope, and we serve him with an undivided heart, or we should do so."⁸

The promises he made during his missionary labors are interesting, proving that he never wilfully deceived one for any purpose whatsoever: "I have preached in the United States, in the British Provinces, and in the Island of Great Britain, and have invariably promised the Saints one blessing, viz., hard labor, hard fare, and plenty of persecution, if they would only live their religion, and I believe they are generally well satisfied that this promise has been amply fulfilled. If the Saints cannot endure, and endure to the end, they have no reason to expect eternal salvation."⁹

Later in his life he said further on this subject: "When I was in England did I, apart from the Priesthood, exercise an influence over any of your minds to cause you to come here and locate? Was I the instrument that caused you to forsake your friends in your native country, and gather with the Latter-day Saints? Your enemies will tell you that it was the influence that I held over you which prompted your movements; but that is not true. I have no more influence over the Latter-day Saints, aside from the Priesthood, than you have over each other. If the Spirit of truth does not speak through me and dictate my words, they are no

better than the words of another man. If the Holy
Ghost manifests to you, one thousand or ten thousand
miles from here, that this is the time the Lord has
fixed for building up his Zion—that this is the time
spoken of by the Prophets in which the Saints are
commanded to gather out from the wicked, then it is the
Spirit of the Most High that has influenced and controlled you, and not me nor any other man."[10]

The end of Brigham's direct missionary experience
occurred when in April, 1841, he left England. On July
1st with Heber C. Kimball, and John Taylor he arrived
in Nauvoo. There was great rejoicing amongst the
people at their return, and from the Prophet they received their welcome, "Well done!" Soon after this the
Prophet received a revelation concerning Brigham's missionary labors (as recorded in the Doctrine and Covenants Section 126) in which it is told that his labor was
accepted and he was directed to remain at home. Thus
were his great gifts and talents turned into other channels.

The secret of the great sacrifice made by this good
man and others who have left all to follow the Master
he explained in his later life: "When I left my family to
start for England, I was not able to walk one mile,
I was not able to lift a small trunk, which I took with
me, into the wagon. I left my wife and my six children
without a second suit to their backs, for we had left
all our property in possession of the mob. Every one of
my family was sick, and my youngest child, who has
spoken before you today, was but ten days old at the
time I left for England. Joseph said, 'If you will go, I
promise you, that your family shall live, and you shall
live, and you shall know that the hand of God is in
calling you to go and preach the Gospel of life and sal-

vation to a perishing world.' He said all he could say
to comfort and encourage the brethren. This was our
situation, and I say, with regard to the remainder of
the Twelve, they had all been driven like myself, and
we were a band of brethren about equal. My family
lived. When I left them they had no provisions to last
them ten days, and not one soul of them was able to go
to the well for a pail of water. I had lain for weeks, myself, in the house, watching from day to day for some
person to pass the door, whom I could get to bring us
in a pail of water. In this condition I left my family, and
went to preach the Gospel. As for being cast down, or at
all discouraged, or even such thoughts entering my heart
as 'I will provide for my family, and let the world perish,'
these feelings and thoughts never once occurred to me;
if I had known that every one of them would have been
in the grave when I returned, it would not have diverted
me from my mission one hour. When I was ready to
start, I went and left my family in the hands of the
Lord, and with the brethren.

"I returned again in two years, and found that I
had spent hundreds of dollars, which I had accumulated
on my mission, to help the brethren to emigrate to Nauvoo, and had but one sovereign [$5.00] left. I said I
would buy a barrel of flour with that, and sit down and
eat it with my wife and children, and I determined I
would not ask anybody for work, until I had eaten it all
up. Brother Joseph asked me how I intended to live. I
said, 'I will go to work and get a living.' I tarried in Nauvoo from the year 1841 to 1846, the year we left. In that
time I had accumulated much property, for the Lord mul-
tiplied everything in my hands, and blessed all my undertakings. But I never ceased to preach; and traveled every
season, both in the winter, and in the summer. I was

at home occasionally, and the Lord fed and clothed me. It has never entered into my heart, from the first day I was called to preach the Gospel to this day, when the Lord said, 'Go and leave your family,' to offer the least objection. It has never entered into my heart to violate my covenants, to be an enemy to my neighbor, to deceive, to lie, or to take to myself that which was not my own. The youth around me, in their addresses this day, have eulogized the life and ability of brother Brigham; I want you not only to do as I have done, but a great deal better."[11]

CHAPTER 9

BRIGHAM TAKES THE HELM

WE ARE told that the world needs righteous leaders today more than any other one thing. How may one become a leader? What does it mean to be a leader? May one who has not first learned to be a sincere and willing follower ever become a great leader? These are questions for all to consider.

The stirring scenes of the expulsion from Missouri would cause us to linger, did time permit. Of deep interest are the events leading to the move into Illinois and the Prophet's escape from his foul prison experience. Th story of the purchase of the townsite of Commerce on the Mississippi River and the draining of it to make the land habitable for man's abode forms a stirring account of modern land conquest and city planning. In all of this activity Brigham took a leading part, since at that time through the course of events he had become President of the Quorum of the Twelve Apostles. He was ever and always the Prophet's "right hand man" and in these trying experiences was learning many lessons that he would find invaluable later on.

Keys pass to the Twelve. It would seem to the student of history that for the last few years of his life the Prophet knew that his earthly mission was nearly complete. He often called the Twelve together, telling them that "they now had the keys of the new dispensation."

We read from Tullidge: "The Prophet had now nearly reached the zenith of his power. His marvelous career was drawing to a close. But he had lived long enough to see his mission planted firmly in the United States and Europe. He had seen, too, the very man rise by his side who, perhaps, above all men in the world, was the one

most fitted in every respect to succeed him and carry the
new dispensation to a successful issue. Every move
which Joseph made from that moment to his death
manifested his instinctive appreciation of that fact. At
the next conference the Prophet called upon the Twelve
to stand in their place and 'bear off the Kingdom of
God' victorious among all nations. From that time, too,
the burden of his sayings was that he was 'rolling off
the kingdom from his own shoulders on to the shoulders
of the Twelve.' The mantle of Joseph was falling upon
Brigham. He lived barely long enough to make this
appreciated, and to prepare the church for his martyrdom. A thousand times did the Prophet foreshadow his
death. Every day he told his people in some form of
the coming event. They blinded their understanding;
yet, today they remember but too well the prophetic
significance which indicated the close of his mortal
career. If any man could have averted the stroke of
fate, that man was Brigham Young. Had he been in
Nauvoo he would have probably prevented the martyrdom. But strange to say, in spite of the foregoing revelation, and Joseph's evident feelings of safety with Brigham by his side, he sent him again on a mission, during
which period the tragedy occurred."[1]

The tragic experiences of the martyrdom of the
Prophet and his loved brother the Patriarch are dark
pages in the history of our fair land, which was dedicated to freedom of every man's religious belief. Brigham had been sent East on a special mission concerning
the coming candidacy of the Prophet as President of
the United States. He was in Boston with Wilford
Woodruff when he received news that the tragedy had
occurred. Indeed, most of the Quorum were scattered
over the country on missionary assignments. Only two

of them were in Nauvoo at the time, John Taylor and Willard Richards, both of whom were in prison with their beloved leaders.

Thus, after fourteen short years of official service, the Prophet's ministry was ended and the new Church had reached the greatest crisis of its history. In spite of the Prophet's warnings the people were actually unprepared for the terrible tragedy which was upon them.

"Very little thought had been given to the subject of succession in the Presidency, even by the leading brethren, for such a contingency seemed to them to be very remote. The revelations were clear on that point, but there had been no consideration of the subject. In the revelation on Priesthood, given to the apostles in 1835 the Lord said that the council of the apostles was equal in authority with the First Presidency, and Joseph Smith stated that its place was second only to the presidency of the Church and where there was no First Presidency, the apostles would preside.[2] When the Saints were left without the guiding hand of the Prophet, they were in confusion, not fully understanding this order of the Priesthood. Sidney Rigdon, first counselor to President Joseph Smith, had lost the spirit of the work. Contrary to the direct command of the Lord in a revelation[3] he moved his residence to Pittsburgh, Pennsylvania, where he was of little assistance as a counselor in the presidency. For many months before his death, Joseph Smith had suspected Sidney Rigdon of being in league with his enemies."[4]

Is it not a queer coincidence that at the time of the martyrdom, both of Joseph's counselors, Sidney Rigdon and William Law, were disaffected and in a state of apostasy, leaving him utterly alone in that presiding quorum? Also that most of the Twelve were scattered over the country?

Brigham's return to Nauvoo with his great sorrow may well be imagined. In writing of this period most Church historians dwell only upon the dramatic events which followed upon the arrival of the Twelve in Nauvoo on August 6, 1844. But the fancy lingers with Brigham Young in the long days which lay between Boston and Nauvoo. He knew that he had been glad to sink his own personality in the absorbing glow which surrounded the first, second and the very last word and act of the Prophet. He was his witness, as Joseph was witness of the Savior. Brigham left to John C. Bennett, to Sidney Rigdon and to William Law, the dramatics and pyrotechnics of public life. He had not been in any sense a dominant Nauvoo figure. President of the Twelve Apostles he was, and so deeply engaged in carrying forward the vast number of mighty projects and plans of his leader that he had no time and less desire to institute any new ones of his own. Thus he proved himself an ideal follower. He found the people not only bowed down with grief but in utter confusion—literally a flock without a shepherd.

As soon as the word of the foul martyrdom of the Prophet Joseph and his beloved brother Hyrum, the Patriarch, reached Sydney Rigdon, he hastened to Nauvoo to claim the leadership of the Church—even though he had been absent from the Church and had entirely lost the spirit of the work. But ambition plays strange tricks on most people. Indeed, at the Prophet's last conference with the Church he desired that Rigdon be not sustained as his counsellor. His brother pleaded for Rigdon, but Joseph remarked: "I have thrown him off my shoulders but you have put him on me; you may

carry him but I will not."⁵ Yet when the crisis came
Rigdon wanted to be the Prophet's successor.

Brigham knew from the Prophet's teaching that
when the President dies or is removed for cause, then
the next quorum in the Church, the Twelve, must assume leadership.

The story of the transfiguration of Brigham as he
stood before the people speaking with the very voice
of Joseph and being a living witness to the hosts assembled that "the mantle of Joseph had fallen upon
Brigham," is a stirring one, full of drama and truth!
President George Q. Cannon who was present as a boy
of twelve years thus records the scene: "It was the
first sound of his [Brigham's] voice which the people
had heard since he had gone east on his mission, and
the effect upon them was most wonderful. Who that
was present on that occasion can ever forget the impression it made upon them? If Joseph had risen from
the dead, and again spoken in their hearing, the effect
could not have been more startling than it was to the
many present at that meeting; it was the voice of Joseph
himself; and not only was it the voice of Joseph which
was heard, but it seemed in the eyes of the people as
though it was the very person of Joseph which stood
before them. The Lord gave his people a testimony that
left no room for doubt, as to who was the man He
had chosen to lead them. They both saw and heard with
their natural eyes and ears; and then the words which
were uttered came, accompanied by the convincing power
of God to their hearts, and they were filled with the
Spirit and with great joy. There had been gloom and
in some hearts, probably doubt and uncertainty; but
now it was plain to all that here was the man upon

whom the Lord had bestowed the necessary authority
to act in their midst in Joseph's stead."[6]

**Thus the mantle of Joseph, the Prophet, fell upon
Brigham** and the people knew in their souls that he
was the leader to succeed their loved and honored Prophet. Brigham's experience on that occasion is interesting.
Among other things he said: "When I came to this
stand I had peculiar feelings and impressions. The faces
of the people seemed to say: 'We want a shepherd to
guide us through this world.' To all who want to draw
away from the Church, I say let them do it if they
choose, but they will not prosper. They will find there
is a power with the Apostles which will carry the work
off victoriously and which will build up and defend the
Church and Kingdom of God in all the world.

"What do the people want? I want the privilege
of weeping and mourning for thirty days at least, and
then rising up and telling the people what the Lord wants
of them. Although my heart is too full of mourning to
launch out into business transactions and into the or-
ganizations of the Church, I feel compelled this day to
step forth and discharge all those duties God had placed
upon me."[7]

Rigdon's claim was that he had been consecrated "a
spokesman unto Joseph" (whatever that might mean),
and was "to be guardian and build the Church up unto
Joseph." His claim was met by Brigham Young's calm
assertion that he did not care who presided over the
Church, even though it were Ann Lee (originator of the
Shaker sect), but he would have to know what the Lord
said about it. "Joseph has conferred upon the heads
of the Twelve," said Brigham, "all the keys and powers
belonging to the Apostleship, and no man or set of men
can get between Joseph and the Twelve in this world

or in the world to come." Yet at this time Brigham made
it very clear that while God designated His Prophet,
the people must decide who was to be their earthly
leader. Here was one of the first and greatest tests of
the noble and God-given doctrine of "common consent,"
enunciated and put into practice by the Prophet himself.

The people were definitely the ones to decide. Did
they want Sidney Rigdon or the Quorum of the Twelve
to lead them now that the First Presidency had been so
tragically disorganized? Their answer was given in no
uncertain terms. The vast majority supported the
Twelve. Only a very small, self-seeking, ambitious minor-
ity held out against them. Indeed, the vote for the
Twelve might be said to have been unanimous.

Thus the second quorum in the Church, not Brigham Young as a man, took the responsibility of leadership as they should, when the first quorum, the First
Presidency, was disorganized. Therefore the Twelve, as
a quorum, governed the Church until December, 1847,
when the First Presidency was reorganized with Brigham Young as President, Heber C. Kimball and Willard
Richards as Counselors.

No one in this Church questions the fact that Brigham Young was a great leader for he demonstrated this
power during all his subsequent active life. It is well-
known also that never in thought, word or deed did he
attempt to take unto himself honor for the accomplishments of his life. First to God, who inspired the Prophet,
and then to Joseph, whose willing disciple Brigham was,
did he give all the credit for his great life work.

The essence of leadership is a quality little understood by most people but well demonstrated in the life

of Brigham Young. Those who have this power pre-
eminently seem to sense instinctively that one who has
never learned to follow, to work side by side with others,
winning their confidence and good will, may never
become a leader. The real leader never domineers or
dominates his fellows; he gains their cooperation and
accepts willingly their counsel when needed, and acts on
all issues of righteousness with their full support. The
other type of leader who rules by force or accumulated
power, disregarding the rights of his fellows, making
his own will dominant, may be an autocrat or dictator
but he is not a real leader of men.

Brigham learned well this lesson. A story is told
of his calling the Twelve together on one occasion (long
before the Prophet's death) to discipline one of its members. The Prophet heard of it and believing the man
innocent, went to the meeting and protested.

"What would you have us do, Brother Joseph?"
said Brigham. "I think you have acted hastily and I
would advise delay," said the Prophet. "This meeting is
dismissed," said Brigham calmly and unperturbed.
"When our file leader speaks we know he is right. When
the time comes for action he will know it as well as we
do." The man was later disfellowshipped, but Brigham
did exactly right.

On countless other occasions he stood back of the
Prophet and was willing in every way to submerge his
own personality in carrying out the Prophet's orders.
The work was greater than he, and he was big enough
to recognize the modern Prophet of God. In nothing
else did Brigham show so well his own great power as
a leader of men.

CHAPTER 10

ORDER OUT OF CHAOS

I N AN institution founded on Truth a new leader does not destroy the work of his predecessor nor try to supplant existing methods with his own. He realizes that progress is a process of growth and that new ideas or methods must be an outgrowth of what has gone before. Thus only may growth be orderly. Brigham understood this truth and practiced it. The Prophet had laid well the foundation stones; his was the task of adding somewhat to the superstructure.

Brigham's powers of leadership were soon sensed by the people. From the hour of his first appeal to the quorums and to the body of the people, he steadily maintained, as he had seen the Prophet do, the delicate balance of power between the divinely ordained authority of the Priesthood, in their several appointments to lead, guide and direct, and the will of each church member to be so governed either in or out of quorums—yea, even to the last member thereof! Each has a right to sustain or reject persons or policies. All men and women appointed to positions of trust and leadership, all policies for public control and government, pertaining to Church guidance, all revelations even, were then and are to this day brought annually or oftener before the congregations of the Saints for their acceptance or rejection. In that choice, the exercise of free agency, man, woman and child receives the blessing if the law is observed, or pays the penalty when the law is disobeyed.

Therefore Church affairs, fluid and chaotic since the martyrdom, were at once taken up, flying ends knitted together in sequence, and the people felt there was a steady hand at the helm of the "Old Ship Zion" which they loved thus to symbolize.

The completion of the Temple seemed to be Brigham's first concern, that it might be dedicated as the Prophet has foretold. Brigham said, "I wish you distinctly to understand that the counsel of the Twelve is for every family that does not belong to the Pine Company to stay in Nauvoo to build the Temple and obtain the endowments to be given therein. Do not scatter. United we stand, divided we fall. If we do not carry out the plan laid down by Joseph we can get no further endowments. I want this to sink deep into your hearts that you may appreciate it.

"Do the people leave home because they are afraid? If so, I tell them before God that they shall have no place to rest, but shall flee from place to place like the Jews. I would rather have the dead body of the Prophet than some men who are alive. We want to build the Temple in this place even if we have to do as the Jews did in their erection of the Temple in Jerusalem: Work with a sword in one hand and a trowel in the other. Stay here. Plow, sow, and build. Put your plow shares into the prairie. One plow share will do more to drive off the mob than two guns. Store your grain in Nauvoo, for it will be needed there while you are building the Temple."

The people rallied to the call of the new leader, and for a time it seemed that a peace and prosperity they had not known for years might be theirs. They were happy in fulfilling all the duties that could be desired of them—that is, those who were righteous did so. But alas, there were wolves within the fold as well as wolves without, as subsequent events proved.

The enemies of the Church who, from the Governor down permitted the mob to butcher innocent men ir cold blood, felt that if they could only kill the Prophet

of the faith, the whole Church would fall to pieces. They
rejoiced at the chaos in which the Church found itself on
the death of its leaders, and hoped it would be permanent and that Mormonism, so-called, would be a thing
of the past. Little did they understand that God and
not man is at the head of this Church, and that, it is
established on earth never more to be thrown down.
Brigham and the Quorum of the Twelve knew that,
none knew it better than they, and that knowledge gave
them courage and the wisdom to proceed in an orderly
fashion to make the Church function as it did in the
Prophet's day.

When these enemies of the people learned that affairs of the Church were prospering and not disintegrat-
ing, they began plotting and devising ways of renew-
ing their vicious attacks. The disgruntled, ambitious
apostates of Nauvoo combined their forces with the
hellish schemes of the mobs without and trouble began
anew.

Remy and Brenchley's pen picture of affairs at that
time is most interesting. These two men, who were
French travelers, visited Salt Lake City at a later
time and were so interested in what they saw they wrote
a book, "A Journey to Great Salt Lake City." From it
we quote; (Vol. I p. 414)

Up to the period when he was called to preside over the
destinies of Mormonism, Brigham had led an exceedingly active
life, and had entirely devoted himself to the defense and propaga-
tion of the new doctrine. He had been constantly employed in
the missions to Canada, to the United States, and to England.
His activity did not decrease in the high position to which he
had risen. All kinds of industry went rapidly ahead, and Nauvoo
very soon recovered its prosperity, counting, towards the month of
December, fourteen thousand inhabitants, of whom about nine-
tenths were Mormons. The Temple progressed, and gave promise

of being a really remarkable structure. Brigham urged above all things that it should be promptly completed. The other public buildings of the city were the Hall of the Seventy, the Masonic Hall, the Social Hall.

Under the vigorous and wise rule of Brigham, the Church began to enjoy somewhat of peace, and the year 1844, which had been so full of storms and calamities, closed, comparatively speaking, in great tranquility. Without, matters proceeded less favorably.

Amid the trickery of their enemies and their own incessant labors, half the year 1845 passed away. However, during their anxieties, the Saints, under Brigham's direction never for a moment ceased their labors, and by the end of May the walls of the temple were completed amid great public rejoicings. The coolness of the faithful disciples of Joseph, and their comparative success, soon gave a finishing touch to the hatred of the "gentiles."

In September they (the mob) burned the houses and property of the Saints who resided in the settlement of Morley. During the day of the 11th of September alone, twenty-nine houses became a prey to the flames, and the unhappy inhabitants were reduced to sleep in the open air under a pelting rain.

The Mormons, however, bore these outrages with resignation; they relied on the support of the law, which was once more to fail them. The storm was not to be allayed. The anti-Mormons—one is surprised to find among them senators, civil and military officers and even clergymen—increased in audacity and numbers in proportion as their savage persecutions augmented. They soon found themselves absolute masters of the position, and on the 22nd of September, 1845, at a meeting held at Quincy, they resolved that the expulsion of the Mormons should be affected at any cost, even by means of force, should persuasion fail. They at once deputed delegates to Nauvoo, charged to communciate to the heads of the Church the resolution made at that meeting. Brigham Young had the good sense to understand that he was in a crisis in which the feeling of the majority supplants law, and that it was henceforth impossible for his people to live in the State. He answered the Quincy deputies, that it was his intention to abandon Illinois the following spring, that was to say, as soon as the Mormons were able to dispose of their

property. This sudden and unexpected determination sufficed, if
not to extinguish, at least to suspend hostilities.

An amusing story of those days (sometimes called
the "Bogus Brigham Story") depicts the feeling of the
enemies of righteousness, as well as Brigham's wisdom
in meeting a crisis. It is told by himself.

I was in my room in the Temple at Nauvoo, after the mur-
der of the Prophet and his brother Hyrum. I learned that a
posse was lurking around the building, and that the United
States Marshal was waiting for me to come down, whereupon
I knelt down and asked my Father in Heaven to guide and
protect me, that I might live to prove advantageous to the
saints. I arose from my knees, and sat down in my chair. There
came a rap at my door. "Come in," I said: and Brother George
D. Grant, who was then engaged driving my carriage and doing
chores for me, entered the room. Said he, "Brother Brigham, do
you know that a posse and the United States Marshal are here?"
I told him I had heard so. On entering the room, Brother Grant
had left the door open. Nothing came into my mind what to
do until looking across the hall I saw Brother William Miller
leaning against the wall. As I stepped towards the door I
beckoned to him; he came. "Brother William," I said, "the Marshal is here for me; will you go and do just as I tell you? If
you will I will serve him a trick." I knew that Brother Miller was
an excellent man, perfectly reliable, capable of carrying out my
project. "Here, take my cloak," said I; but it happened to be
Brother Heber C. Kimball's, our cloaks were alike in colour, fashion
and size. I threw it around his shoulders, and told him to wear
my hat and accompany Brother George D. Grant. He did so.
"George, you step into the carriage," said I to Brother Grant,
"and look towards Brother Miller, and say to him, as though you
were addressing me, 'Are you ready to ride?' You can do this
and they will suppose Brother Miller to be me, and proceed
accordingly." And they did so.

Just as Brother Miller was entering the carriage the Marshal stepped up to him, and placing his hand upon his shoulder,
said, "You are my prisoner." . . . .

When they arrived within two or three miles of Carthage,
the Marshal. with his posse, stopped. They arose in their car-

riages, buggies and wagons, and, like a tribe of Indians going to battle, or as if they were a pack of demons, yelling and shouting, exclaimed: "We've got him! we've got him! we've got him!"

When they reached Carthage, the Marshal took the supposed Brigham into an upper room of the hotel, and placed a guard over him, at the same time telling those around that he had got him. Brother Miller remained in the room until they bid him come to supper. While there, parties came in one after the other, and asked for Brigham. Brother Miller was pointed out to them. So it continued, until an apostate Mormon, by the name of Thatcher, who had lived in Nauvoo, came in, sat down and asked the landlord where Brigham was.

"That is Mr. Young," said the landlord, pointing across the table to Brother Miller.

"Where? I can't see anyone that looks like Brigham," Thatcher replied.

The landlord told him it was that fleshy man, eating.

"Oh," exclaimed Thatcher, "That's not Brigham; that's William Miller, one of my old neighbors."

Upon hearing this the landlord went, and tapping the Marshal on the shoulder, took him a few steps to one side and said:

"You have made a mistake. That is not Brigham Young. It is William Miller of Nauvoo."

The Marshal, very much astonished, exclaimed: "Good Heavens! and he passed for Brigham." He then took Brother Miller into a room, and turning to him said: "Why didn't you tell me your name?"

"You have not asked me my name," Brother Miller replied.

"Well, what is your name?" said the Marshal with an oath.

"My name is William Miller."

The Marshal, in a rage, walked out of the room, followed by Brother Miller who hastened away to a place of safety.[1]

Why were the people persecuted is a question that might well be asked again. Surely if they were honest and law-abiding they should be safe anywhere then as now. One is apt to think that "where there was so much smoke there must have been some fire." What really was the cause of so much hatred and ill treatment?

Unquestionably there must have been some members of the Church who were dictatorial and quarrelsome. No one may ever claim that the "Mormons" were or are perfect, since they are human. Yet it is unquestionably true that they could not possibly have merited the horrible persecution which was heaped upon them, for the huge majority were honest, peace-loving and law-abiding. Brigham later made the statement: "Although there was so much opposition and persecution carried on against the Saints in Missouri, I never knew a Latter-day Saint to break a law while I was there; and if the records of Clay, Caldwell, or Daviess Counties were searched, they could not find one record of crime against one of our brethren, or even in Jackson County so far as I know."

Why then, the hatred? The Prophet Joseph answers the question for all time. In an address to the Nauvoo Legion on June 18, 1844, he said: "It is thought by some that our enemies would be satisfied with my destruction; but I tell you that as soon as they have shed my blood, they will thirst for the blood of every man in whose heart dwells a single spark of the spirit of the fulness of the Gospel. The opposition of these men is moved by the spirit of the adversary of all righteousness. It is not only to destroy me, but every man and woman who dares believe the doctrines that God hath inspired me to teach to this generation."[2]

Add to this fundamental reason the fact that the Mormons were Abolitionists while many of the other people at that time were slave holders, as well as the fact that politically the Mormons might be counted on to vote as a unit, and one has a fair idea of the religious-political opposition of those who prefer darkness rather than light.

Brigham Young understood well the causes of the opposition, yet sought by every laudable means in his power to gain the support of his state and nation to invoke the law in the protection of the people who had been so grossly maligned and persecuted. He sent petitions to the Governor and even to the President of the United States, but all to no avail—not one word was ever received in reply. The people must depend upon themselves and their God alone for succor and protection. Their loved Government had cast them out and appeared to care naught for their welfare. They were outcasts indeed.

As Brigham's loyalty and devotion to his leader and friend "Brother Joseph" constitutes an enduring testimony to the overwhelming quality of Joseph's personality, so, too, did the willingness of Brigham Young's powerful associates to accept his leadership manifest the dominating quality of "Brother Brigham's" own character and ability. Most men and women are followers. They seek out sub-consciously a dominant, persuasive master-mind. But to unite a group of powerful, magnetic, individualistic men and women into one acquiescent body—and under such circumstances as confronted panic-stricken Nauvoo—this was the task for a Moses.

Yet Brigham Young, then or ever, took no credit, assumed no role of superiority; he was merely the spokesman of the people and the medium through whom God might communicate His will to His children on earth.

The results of this divinely constituted organization, the effects of power, unity, self-control and group-sanity, not only became speedily apparent in Nauvoo, but were and are written on every page of subsequent Church history, as well as in the self-reliant and virtuous characters of the fourth, fifth, sixth, and even seventh generations of the founders' descendants. The people were united, and a real leader was with them to point the way out of their many difficulties.

CHAPTER 11.

"GO WEST, YOUNG MAN"

THE harassed leaders knew by the autumn of 1845 that it was impossible to remain longer in Illinois. The oppressive yell of the mob, who tormented helpless women and sometimes killed men and cattle, filled the surrounding country with terror. Government officials themselves warned Brigham to flee. Governor Ford obtained a promise from him and the leaders that they would evacuate Nauvoo in the spring of 1846. Ford wrote to President Young in April, 1845, advising him "to get off by yourselves where you can enjoy peace." His advice, while it fitted in with future plans, was not needed. Brigham Young was well aware of the prophecy of Joseph Smith concerning the Rocky Mountains and he knew what the ancient prophets had foretold. Therefore, he needed not the spur of Ford's cowardly urging. They would eventually settle in the Rocky Mountains. But where, and how was it to be done?

Consultation and deep study as well as prayer and preparation must precede action. Remy and Brenchley tell us: "At the conference which was held the 6th of October under the unfinished roof of the temple, the principal part of the preachers spoke of the means of effecting the projected emigration. Lyman Wight had proposed Texas, where, in fact, he had himself gone after his excommunication; John Taylor had indicated Vancouver's Island; others were in favor of California. After a long but calm debate, wherein they carefully weighed the advantages and disadvantages of each of the proposed places, it was resolved that they should go and settle in some valley in the Rocky Mountains."

This is a striking evidence of the wisdom of Brigham Young thus early in his career, to encourage free dis-

cussion of the place where they should finally settle.
Yet he knew, for Joseph had announced the place they
were to go; and when all were through with their discussion, Brigham's calm words carried the day. It was
in the Rocky Mountains that the new Zion should arise!

That the leaders were not setting out blindly is well-
known. They studied any and all available material that
would give them definite information. The manuscript
Church History reports: "Nauvoo Temple—20th of December, 1845. This was a beautiful morning in Nauvoo.
President Brigham Young dictated the arrangements of
the day. Afterwards with a few of the Twelve and others,
he heard Franklin D. Richards read **Fremont's Journal,**
giving an account of his travels in California."

Heber C. Kimball's journal also notes: "Nauvoo
Temple, December 31, 1845. President Young and myself are superintending the operations of the day, ex-
amining maps with reference to selecting a location in
the Rocky Mountains, and reading the various works
which have been written and published by travelers in
these regions."

The periodicals of the day, especially **The Nauvoo
Neighbor,** were full of accounts of conditions in the
Western and Pacific United States. The leaders were
close students of the accounts of Freemont, Hastings,
and other western travelers.

The people hurried their preparation as much as
possible, yet the fiends who persecuted them were so insistent that they were forced to leave in the dead of
winter, whether or not they were prepared. That page
of United States history is well-known and its cruelty
has scarcely ever had a parallel.

On a Wednesday, February 4, 1846, the first group
of people left their homes, their gardens—the fruit of

years of toil and struggle—with their few most necessary provisions packed in hastily prepared wagons, to find new homes at an unknown destination. Other groups followed and on February 15 the leaders, Brigham Young, Willard Richards, and George A. Smith with a large company began the journey by crossing the huge Mississippi river which was then completely frozen over.

The story of the expulsion of a multitude of peace-loving people unprotected and unprepared, over the frozen rivers and prairies, and later in the year through bogs and swamps of an uncharted and uninhabited country, is one that seems difficult to understand today. It was the intention to leave temporary settlements at Mount Pisgah and Garden Grove, Iowa, and Council Bluffs or Winter Quarters, on the banks of the Missouri River, as the body of the Saints moved on West in the spring of 1846. But this plan was greatly handicapped. A testing time was at hand! It is one thing to possess loyal sentiments; it is quite another matter to throw them into the crucible of action.

The United States Government was asked through the people's representative in the East, Mr. Jesse A. Little, to help them make this westward journey, since they could not be protected in their homes.

Tyler's History of the Mormon Battalion (p. 111) states that: "Oregon at that time was in possession of the United States, and President Polk had recommended to Congress that stockade forts be built along the overland route to that distant part, as a protection to emigrants. In anticipation of a law being passed to this effect, the Saints endeavored to secure the work of building the forts. They knew they could do the work as well and as cheaply as any others, as they expected to

travel some distance in that direction. Besides, the
means to be earned by such work would greatly aid
in supporting them; and the fact of their being in the
employ of the Government might serve as a guaranty
of their good faith.

"In alluding to this, in a circular issued by the
High Council, at Nauvoo, January 20, 1846, it was stated
that, 'Should hostilities arise between the Government of
the United States and any other power, in relation to the
right of possessing the territory of Oregon we are on
hand to sustain the United States government to that
country. It is geographically ours; and of right no foreign
power should hold dominion there; and if our services
are required to prevent it, those services will be cheer-
fully rendered according to our ability.' "

It is true that Mr. Little had been asked by President Young to accept any honorable means of help
offered by the Government, and it may be that since
the war with Mexico had arisen he thought that the
enlistment of the Mormon men would aid the people
in their journey west. It is certain, however, that the
motive of all the national leaders was not so altruistic,
and it is more certain that an order calling for the
majority of their young and able-bodied men came to
the people as a crushing blow.

The call for the Mormon Battalion, which came in
June, 1846, was therefore most unexpected. The leaders
who had made the request of the Government never
dreamed of having their young man-power moving off
under martial orders, leaving their families to the mercies
of an already overburdened people in exile.

Let Brigham himself tell this story: "Permit me to
draw your attention, for a moment, to a few facts in
relation to raising the Battalion for the Mexican war.

When the storm cloud of persecution lowered down upon us on every side, when every avenue was closed against us, our Leaders treacherously betrayed and slain by the authorities of the Government in which we lived, and no hope of relief could penetrate through the thick darkness and gloom which surrounded us on evey side, no voice was raised in our behalf, and the General Government was silent to our appeals. When we had been insulted and abused all the day long, by those in authority requiring us to give up our arms, and by every other act of insult and abuse which the prolific imagination of our enemies could devise to test, as they said, our patriotism (which requisitions, be it known, were always complied with on our part), and when we were finally compelled to flee, for the preservation of our lives and the lives of our wives and children to the wilderness; I ask, had we not reason to feel that our enemies were in the ascendant? that even the government, by their silent acquiescence, were also in favor of our destruction? Had we not, I ask, some reason to consider them all, both the people and the Government alike, our enemies?

"And when, in addition to all this, and while fleeing from our enemies, another test of fidelity and patriotism was contrived by them for our destruction and acquiesced in by the Government, consisting of a requisition from the War Department, to furnish a Battalion of five hundred men to fight under their officers, and for them, in the war then existing with Mexico, I ask again, could we refrain from considering both people and Government our most deadly foes? Look a moment at our situation, and the circumstances under which this requisition was made. We were migrating, we knew not whither, except that it was our intention to go beyond the reach of our enemies. We had no homes, save our

wagons and tents, and no stores of provisions and clothing; but had to earn our daily bread by leaving our
families in isolated locations for safety, and going among
our enemies to labor. Were we not, even before this
cruel requisition was made, unmercifully borne down
by oppression and persecution past endurance by any
other community? But under these trying circumstances
we were required to turn out of our traveling camps
500 of our most efficient men, leaving the old, the young
and the women upon the hands of the residue, to take
care of and support; and in case we refused to comply
with so unreasonable a requirement, we were to be
deemed enemies to the Government, and fit only for
the slaughter.

"Look also at the proportion of the number required
of us, compared with that of any other portion of the
Republic. A requisition of only thirty thousand from
a population of more than twenty millions was all that
was wanted, and more than was furnished, amounting
to only one person and a half to a thousand inhabitants.
If all other circumstances had been equal, if we could
have left our families in the enjoyment of peace, quiet-
ness, and security in the houses from which we had been
driven, our quota of an equitable requisition would not
have exceeded four persons. Instead of this, five hundred
must go, thirteen thousand percent above an equal ratio,
even if all other things had been equal, but under the
peculiar circumstances in which it was made, comparison fails to demonstrate, and reason itself totters
beneath its enormity.

"And for whom were we to fight? As I have already shown, for those that we had every reason to
believe were our most deadly foes. Could the Government have expected our compliance therewith? Did

they expect it? Did not our enemies believe that we would spurn, with becoming resentment and indignation, such an unhallowed proposition? And were they not prepared to make our rejection of it a pretext to inflame the Government still more against us, and thereby accomplish their hellish purposes upon an innocent people, in their utter extinction?

"**How was this proposition received,** and how was it responded to by this people? I went myself, in company with a few of my brethren, between one and two hundred miles along the several routes of travel, stopping at every little camp, using our influence to obtain volunteers, and on the day appointed for the rendezvous the required complement was made up; and this was all accomplished in about twenty days from the time that the requisition was made known.

"Here permit me to pay a tribute of respect to the memory of Captain Allen, the bearer of this requisition from the Government. He was a gentleman full of human feelings, and, had he been spared, would have smoothed the path, and made easy the performance of this duty, so far as laid in his power. His heart was wrung with sympathy when he saw our situation, and filled with wonder when he witnessed the enthusiastic patriotism and ardor which so promptly complied with his requirement; again proving, as we had hundreds of times before proved, by our acts, that we were as ready, and even more so than any other inhabitants of the Republic, to shoulder the musket, and go forth to fight the battles of our common country, or stand in her defense. History furnishes no parallel, either of the severity and injustice of the demand, or in the alacrity, faithfulness and patriotism with which it was answered and complied. Thus can we cite instance after instance of persons holding legal authority, being moved upon, through the misrepresentation and influence of our enemies to insult us as a people, by requiring a test of our patriotism. How long must this state of things continue? So long as the people choose to remain in wilful ignorance with regard to us; so long as they choose to misinterpret our views, misrepresent our feelings, and misunderstand our policy."[1]

The view of an avowed enemy of the Church is interesting. Governor Edwards of Missouri wrote to the Secretary of War, William L. Marcy, the following: "The Mormons are a bad and deluded sect, and they have been harshly treated; but I suppose very correctly; yet they do not believe so, and under the treatment which they have received, if they are not enemies, both of our people and our government, then they are better Christians and purer patriots than other denominations, a thing which nobody in the west can believe."[2]

We do know that in every crisis Brigham Young and the people proved their loyalty and patriotism to their loved country, and may well claim the honor of being "better Christians and purer patriots" than were their enemies.

Brigham's final reaction to the demand and the ready response of the loyal refugees who listened to their country's call fill us with a just pride in their patriotism. During the difficult time of preparation he said: "Do not mention families today; we want to conform to the requisition made upon us and we will do nothing else until we accomplish this thing. If we want the privilege of going where we can worship God according to-the dictates of our conscience, we must raise the Battalion. I say, it is right, and who cares for sacrificing our comforts for a few years? I want to say to every man, the Constitution of the United States, as framed by our fathers, was dictated by the revelations of Jesus Christ, and I tell you in the name of Jesus Christ, it is as good as ever I could ask for. I say unto you, magnify the laws. There is no law in the United States, or in the Constitution, but I am ready to make honorable."[3]

In giving instructions to the members of the Battalion before their departure, President Young requested that they prove themselves to be the best soldiers in the service of the United States. His timely advice was: "Captains, act as fathers to your companies. Manage your men and control yourselves by the power of the Priesthood. Keep yourselves neat and clean in appearance. Observe strict chastity. Be civil and genteel in all your dealings with each other and with all men. No swearing must be allowed, and insult no man, no matter what your provocation may be. Avoid contention with the Missourians, or any other class of people. Take with you your Bibles and Books of Mormon but do not seek to impose your views or religion upon others. Card-playing should not be allowed. Burn any cards you may find, if they belong to our own boys. If you keep these counsels no blood will be shed. See that you do so. After your labors, you will probably be discharged within eight hundred miles of the proposed settlement of the Saints in the Great Basin, where the next Temple will be built in a stronghold free from mobs."[4]

An account of the farewell celebration before the departure of the Battalion is given by Colonel Thomas L. Kane (a friend of the harrassed people), who was present at the time of the final muster. This gives a touching picture of the bravery and wisdom which were necessary to carry the people through this trying ordeal. It also furnishes a perfect conception of the part played by music and social contact in the lives of these God-fearing refugees.

Mr. Kane describes these events:

A central mass meeting for council, some harrangues at the remotely scattered camps, an American flag brought out from the store-house of things rescued and hoisted to the top of a tree mast, and in three days the force was reported, mustered, organized and ready to march. There was no sentimental affection in their leave-taking. It was the custom, whenever the larger camps rested for a few days together, to make great arbors or "boweries" as they called them, or poles and brush and wattling as places of shelter for their meetings of devotion or conference. In one of these, where the ground had been trodden firm and hard by the wor-shippers, was gathered now the mirth and beauty of the Mormon Israel. If anything told that the Mormons had been bred to other lives it was the appearance of the women as they assembled here. Before their flight they had sold their watches and trinkets as the most available resource for raising ready money; and hence, like their partners, who wore waistcoats cut with useless watch pockets, they, although their ears were pierced and bore the marks of rejected pendants, were without earrings, chains or broaches. Except such ornaments, however, they lacked noth-ing most becoming the attire of decorous maidens. The neatly darned white stockings and clean white petticoat, the clear starched collar and chemisette, the somewhat faded, only be-cause too well washed, lawn or gingham gown that fitted modestly to the waist of its pretty wearer—these, if any of them spoke of poverty, spoke of a poverty that had known better days.

With the rest, attended the elders of the Church within call, including nearly all the chiefs of the High Council, with their wives and children. They, the gravest and most trouble-worn, seemed the most anxious of any to be the first to throw off the burden of heavy trouble and thoughts. Their leading and dancing in a great double cotillion, was the signal which bade the festivity commence. To the canto of debonnair violins, the cheer of horns, the jingle of sleigh bells, and the jovial snoring of the tam-bourine, they did dance! None of your minuets or other mortuary processions of gentles in ettiquette, tight shoes, and pinching gloves, but the spirited scientific displays of our venerated and merry grandparents, who were not above following the fiddle to the Fox-chase Inn, or Gardens of Gray's Ferry, Fench Fours, Copenhagen jigs, Virginia reels, and the like forgotten figures executed with the spirit of people too happy to be slow, or bashful, or constrained. Light hearts, blithe figures, and light feet, had it their own way from an early hour till after the sun had dipped behind the sharp sky-line of the Omaha hills. Silence was then called, and a well cultivated Mezzo-soprano voice, belonging to a young lady with fair face and dark eyes, gave with quartette accompaniment a little song, the notes of which I have been unsuccessful in repeated efforts to obtain since—a version of the text, touching to all earthly wanderers:

"By the rivers of Babylon we sat down and wept.

We wept when we remembered Zion."

There was danger of some expression of feeling when the song was over, for it had begun to draw tears! but breaking the quiet with his hard voice, an Elder asked the blessing of Heaven on all who, with purity of heart and brotherhood of spirit, had mingled in that society, and then all dispersed, hastening to cover from the falling dews. All, I remember, but some splendid Indians, who in cardinal scarlet blankets and feathered leggings, had been making foreground figures for the dancing rings, like those in Mr. West's picture of our Philadelphia Treaty, and staring their inability to comprehend the wonderful performances. These loitered to the last, as if unwilling to seek their abject homes.

Well as I knew the peculiar fondness of the "Mormons" for music, their orchestra in service on this occasion astonished me by its numbers and fine drill. The story was that an eloquent Mormon missionary had converted its members in a body at an English town, a stronghold of the sect, and that they took up their trumpets, trombones, drums, and hautboys together, and followed him to America.

When the refugees from Nauvoo were hastened to part with their table ware, jewelry, and almost every other fragment of metal wealth they possessed that was not iron, they had never a thought of giving up the instruments of this favorite band. And when the battalion was enlisted, some of the performers being asked to accompany it, they all refused. Their fortunes went with the Camp of the Tabernacle. They had led the Farewell Service

in the Nauvoo Temple. Their office now was to guide the monster
choruses and Sunday hymns; and like the trumpets of silver,
made of a whole piece, "for the calling of the assembly, and for
the journeying of the camp," to knoll the people into church.
Some of their wind instruments, indeed, were uncommonly full
and pure-toned, and in that clear dry air could be heard to a
great distance. It had the strangest effect in the world, to
listen to their sweet music winding over the uninhabited country.
Something in the style of a Moravian death-tune blown at
day-break, but altogether unique. It might be when you were
hunting a ford over the Great Platte, the dreariest of all wild
rivers, perplexed among the far-reaching sand bars, and curlew
shallows of the shifting bed;—the wind rising would bring you
the first faint thought of a melody; and as you listened, borne
down upon the gust that swept past you a cloud of the dry
sifted sands, you recognized it—perhaps a home-loved theme of
Henry Proch or Mendelssohn—Bartholdy, away out there in the
Indian Marshes![5]

Helen Mar Whitney's journal also gives a most interesting inside picture of that occasion: "Here we met our
staunch young friend Col. Kane, who came to our camp
on the 12th day of July and made a speech concerning
the recruiting orders given by Capt. Allen to raise a
regiment of volunteers for the war against Mexico. Monday, July 20th, was the farewell ball, so touchingly referred to by Col. Kane in the sketch he wrote to the Historical Society of Pennsylvania. We couldn't all go to
the camp where the ball was given, there were not
horses enough; so we who remained had a great feast
and dance of our own, as we could furnish our own
music: so the boys gathered a lot of brush for the bon-
fire in front of our tents and we all prepared for the
celebration. We commenced dancing about noon, stopped
for our feast and then continued our dancing until 10
p.m. Horace, excelled as a flutist and the sweet strains
that flowed soft and mellow from his instrument was
due much to his father's training. One of the songs we

love to hear Bro. Kay sing was 'The Jewish Maid'; his
singing was always an inspiration to us."[6]

Brigham Young's direction of a moving multitude
was masterful. There were refugees from the farthest
outposts of civilization, also the families of the Battalion
boys who had left the camps, now needing greater care,
with the thousands moving west into the Unknown on the
unbroken trails of Iowa; and other thousands in temporary camps at Winter Quarters, Garden Grove and Mount
Pisgah. No father felt a keener solicitude for his infant
than the Leader felt for that hapless host of men, strong
or weak; women, courageous or afraid of the unknown
tomorrow; and the little hungry, adventure-seeking children who neither feared or doubted God and their fathers.
Brigham had them all on the altar of his heart and he
loved them as they loved him. Food, shelter, protection,
these were problems that needed both faith and works.
Patriotism to country was also a vital need.

Brigham Young and the pioneers bore their country's flag in their wagons across the American deserts.
It was the sign and symbol of theri loyalty to their country and of God's protecting wings over-shadowing them.
They were loyal and had proved their patriotism.

CHAPTER 12.

AS COMMONWEALTH ENGINEER

NO MAN or set of men of their own power and strength could have led so successfully the thousands of stricken Saints in their weary march across the half of a continent as did Brigham Young and his sturdy associates. Had they not been definitely guided by an overruling Providence the task had been impossible. The job that lay before them as they faced the uncharted West, beset as they were with possible dangers on every side from Indians, starvation and pestilence, was almost superhuman in its magnitude. Was there ever in history a similar undertaking so successfully completed?

The loss of the 500 fine young men who composed the Mormon Battalion was a great blow to the already stricken people. That and other unforseen events caused a delay of the great body of the people in different camps along the route. It was thus impossible to continue the journey into the Rocky Mountains before winter set in. Therefore they must find some suitable place to spend the winter and prepare for the final journey in the early spring. A place on the west bank of the Missouri River on the lands of the Pottawattamie Indians was chosen. Permission was obtained for the settlement and the camp called Winter Quarters was established. The winter was severe and many deaths of young and old resulted from poor nutrition and other hardships. The people as a whole were busy and happy in preparation for the final journey which was to begin in the early spring of 1847.

The story of the exodus of modern Israel and their settlement (July 24, 1847) in the heart of the Great American Desert is an epic worthy the pen of a Milton or a Shakespeare; for every day of the journey was so full of drama or tragedy that its like has never been told. Everyone must be stirred by the events of the trek across the plains and the settlement of a multitude in a hitherto barren desert.

President George A. Smith, the Church Historian, in a sermon preached many years later described these early events: "We look around today and behold our city clothed with verdure and beautiful with trees and flowers, with streams of water running in almost every direction, and the question is frequently asked, 'How did you ever find this place?' I answer, we were led to it by the inspiration of God. After the death of Joseph Smith, when it seemed as if every trouble and calamity had come upon the Saints, Brigham Young, who was President of the Twelve, then the presiding Quorum of the Church, sought the Lord to know what they should do, and where they should lead the people for safety, and while they were fasting and praying daily on this subject, President Young had a vision of Joseph Smith, who showed him the 'mountain that we now call Ensign Peak, immediately north of Salt Lake City, and there was an ensign fell upon that peak, and Joseph said, 'Build under the point where the colors fall and you will prosper and have peace.' The Pioneers had no pilot or guide, none among them had ever been in the country or knew anything about it. However, they traveled under the direction of President Young until they reached this valley. When they entered it, President Young pointed to that peak, and said he, 'I want to go there.' He went up to the point and said, 'This is Ensign Peak. Now, brethren, organize your exploring parties, so as to be safe from Indians; go and explore where you will, and you will come back every time and say this is the best place.' They accordingly started out exploring companies and visited what we now call Cache, Malad, Tooele, and Utah valleys and other parts of the country in various directions, but all came back and declared this was the best spot."[1]

The trials of early settlement were many and some were dramatic. During the first winter in the Valley food was scarce and it required much sacrifice to save enough grain for planting the next spring. The people were confronted with the query: Would crops grow in this desert waste or would the dire prophecy of Bridger and other trappers (that grain could not be matured in these mountain valleys) be realized? But their leader had faith—so must they.

Then when the crops were their most luscious green in the next spring, came the horrible hordes of huge black crickets to devour every green thing in sight. All human exertion was powerless to stay the destruction. Then after earnest and desperate prayer from all the people, came the flocks of sea gulls to devour the crickets, then to disgorge and go back to devour some more. Surely this was a miracle—for their crops were saved and their faith justified.

Many other trials were met and conquered, not the least of which was the constant menace of the red men, or Indians, whose lands were being pre-empted by the pioneers. Many dramatic and some tragic experiences were endured, in spite of Brigham's advice to "Feed the Indians, don't fight them."

During the first two years over 5,000 people had arrived in "The Valley" and this number was being constantly increased. Naturally, the problems of settlement were legion and were met bravely by these hardy Pioneers.

Soon after the settlement of what is now Salt Lake City, scouts were sent out to all the surrounding country and people followed to make permanent homes in all the valleys where soil and water made such settlements possible. Thus were founded many towns and villages from Canada to Mexico.

As irrigation engineer Brigham probably rendered his greatest material service to the new commonwealth, for without an understanding of the use of water in an arid region, life in the desert would not be possible. The Pioneers never did claim to have discovered the possibility of irrigating arid lands, for the practice of irrigation is as old as civilization. Indeed, the greatest nations of the ancient world have flourished in countries of low rainfall that depended upon irrigation for the production of crops.

However, the practice of irrigation in the modern world is of recent origin. True, the Spanish missions founded here and there in Mexico and California, carried water to their small farms during the heat of summer. The contribution of the Mormon Pioneers is something quite different. They developed methods whereby the practice of irrigation was made possible to hundreds and thousands of farms under the conditions of modern civilization; in fact they founded an entire civilization "under the ditch." Therefore it may be said that the Mormon Pioneers founded modern Anglo-Saxon irrigation practice, and the methods which they developed under stress of necessity and good common sense have been adopted wherever necessary throughout the agricultural world today.

Where did the Pioneers learn about the science of Irrigation? It is well-known that before they left Nauvoo they knew from their study of all available reports and books on the subject the barren nature of the country they hoped to reclaim. In his journal Brigham records: "February 26, 1847. Winter Quarters. I spent the afternoon and evening in council with Elders H. C. Kimball, O. Pratt, E. T. Benson, W. Woodruff, Geo. A. Smith, A. Lyman, N. K. Whitney, William Clayton and J. M. Grant. Conversation ensued relative to journey westward, the construction of boats, traveling, location, seeds, **irrigation science,** etc." In the minutes of a meeting held on the following day occurs this sentence: "We have to seach for land that can be irrigated."[2]

That does not sound as though they picked up the idea of irrigation from the returning Battalion Boys or others who in turn had picked up their knowledge from some scattered Spanish missions. These stalwart pioneers were men who studied and prepared themselves for their task in every conceivable way, and then worked diligently and trusted God for the increase. They succeeded and thereby laid a sure foundation of crop production for this great inland empire.

A prophecy on this subject is now being considered and is fulfilled in part. Said Brigham: "In behalf of the people that live here, and of more that would like to come here, had you more water, I will state that I am fully satisfied that a portion of Weber river can be brought above this place, and thousands of acres of good land rendered susceptible of cultivation."[3] And again, this one yet to come: "When we first came here we had not been two weeks on this square, before the Big Cottonwood canal which we are now building, was just as visible to me as it ever will be when it is completed, and you will yet see boats on it. It has to be there."[4]

Other developments of the new commonwealth are interesting. Brigham was exceedingly anxious that the people should become independent of their neighbors a thousand miles on each side of them. The community should be developed in every particular if they were to become an independent economic group.

According to the United States census returns for the year 1850, the population of the valley of Great Salt Lake numbered 11,354 persons, of whom about 53 per cent were males. There were 6,000 residents in Salt Lake City. There were 16,333 acres under cultivation, on which were raised 128,711 bushels of grain. The value of livestock was estimated at $546,698, and of farming implements at $84,288. And this only three years after the people had settled on what was thought to be an irredeemable desert.

After five years had elapsed from the day the pioneer band entered the valley of Great Salt Lake, the settlers found themselves amidst plenty and comfort in the land of promise, where until their arrival, a human being was seldom seen, save the Indians whose clothing was the skins of rabbits and whose food was roasted crickets. There was no destitution in their midst; there was little sickness.

The trades and industries of those early days included all kinds of work in flour mills, saw mills, lath and planing mills, wagon shops, stone quarries, lime kilns, brick yards, woolen mills, potteries, tanneries, carpets, yarn and hosiery, paper, cement, brooms, soap, glue, etc., brushes, willow-ware, charcoal, coke, coal, salt, ice, fire brick, hats, caps, straw braids, and even artificial flowers.

Other activities also occupied their attention. Mr. Tullidge states: "In the interests of his people he [Brigham Young] became a chief contractor in building the Utah end of the Pacific Railroads; he hastened to con-

struct the Utah Central; he is pushing railroads all over
the Territory. Even before the building of these roads
he had net-worked the settlements with lines of telegraph.
He has been as successful as a railroad king as he was in
leading the Mormons to these valleys. It is not the Wal-
ker Brothers, not the Gentiles, not the 'Apostles,' not
Congress, not the civilization that came from abroad as
an invader, but Brigham Young and the Mormons, who
have given to Utah her railroads and telegraphs. In this,
as also in his social and co-operative experiments, he has
succeeded as far as developed."[5]

The encouragement of home industry is another
proof of Brigham's greatness as an empire builder as
well as a great religious leader. Again quoting Tullidge:
"It has been a cardinal principle with the Mormon people
and the continued counsel and practice of their leaders,
that all articles of consumption should, as speedily as
possible, when practicable, be made at home. No sounder
principle of political economy was ever promulgated.
It was early evident, also, that indiscriminate and un-
controlled importation was not the way to encourage
home production; therefore, if importation could be
canvassed and judiciously guarded, every struggling enterprise at home would be aided; and as soon as supplies
were equal to the demand, these products could be dis-
tributed to every settlement throughout the mountains.
This was the key to the situation; and among the first
results of the idea was the increased manufacture of
jeans, cotton yarns from home-grown cotton, boots and
shoes, clothing, brooms, soap, trunks, leather and other
articles giving employment to many, and opening up
that best of all markets—a home demand for home production."[6]

In his sermons Brigham dwells again and again upon the dignity of labor, the uncertain value of piling up individual wealth and the menace to society when individuals control, through capital, the resources of the community. He knew, none better, the natural tendency of man to provide for self and self alone. He knew also that only through a pure love of God can men truly love one another and seek righteously to help one another as God is willing to help all His children.

Said he on this subject: "The Saints in these mountains are a stalwart athletic people. They have a great capital of bone, muscle and sinew on hand. When this is not employed in the establishment and maintenance of various industries, in prudent, economical labor (the employed doing justice to the employer, working to do good for their own benefit, and the benefit of the Kingdom of God), gathering around them in abundance the comforts of life, the great capital which God has given them as individuals and as a people is wasted.

"The work of building up Zion is in every sense a practical work; it is not a mere theory. A theoretical religion amounts to very little real good or advantage to any person. To possess an inheritance in Zion or in Jerusalem only in theory—only in imagination—would be the same as having no inheritance at all. It is necessary to get a deed of it, to make an inheritance practical, substantial and profitable. Then let us not rest contented with a mere theoretical religion, but let it be practical, self-purifying and self-sustaining, keeping the love of God within us, walking by every precept, by every law, and by every word that is given to lead us. * * * The religion of Jesus Christ is a matter-of-fact religion, and taketh hold of the every-day duties and realities of this life."[7]

The founding of cooperative movements throughout the Church with the organization of Zion's Co-operative Mercantile Institutions is noteworthy, and should have more time for discussion; also the establishment of mills for the manufacture of all necessary commodities. The ideals of cooperation underlying their establishment are fundamental to human welfare.

Immigration from the East and from Europe was encouraged, and a fund called the **Perpetual Emigration Fund** was established whereby those of little means might be helped to make the long journey. Then when established they were to return the money to the fund to assist others. This entailed a stupendous problem in assisting them to become independent after their arrival. Thousands of people availed themselves of these opportunities, and today our people are composed of representatives from many of the nations of the earth. That one fact should and does give great strength and virility to the people.

The formation of a bureau for the purpose of helping these people to find work, known as The Public Works, was undertaken and operated with great success. Brigham himself seemed to be a master of the problem of finding the right job for the right man, or as he termed it, "putting round pegs in round holes and square pegs in square holes." This procedure has now been reduced to a science called vocational guidance. Brigham did not know it by name but he was past-master in its operation. Naturally, the people became useful and therefore successful and happy.

How practical was his advice on these subjects and how applicable to our present conditions! He said: "Put a community in possession of knowledge by means of which they can obtain what they need by the labor of their bodies, and their brains, then, instead of being paupers they will be free, independent and happy, and these distinctions of classes will cease, and there will be but one class, one grade, one great family.

"Do you wish to possess enlarged influence in a political point of view? Gather around you the poor and honest of mankind and bestow your charity on them, not by giving them in the way that charity is almost universally understood, but supply them labor that will pay an interest on the outlay of means and, at the same time, afford food, raiment, and shelter to the laborer; in this way the man of means becomes a benefactor to his race."[8]

The two most fundamental economic principles practiced by this great Commonwealth Engineer should receive consideration. First and most important probably was this advice: **Cultivate the soil,** develop your agriculture and make it the backbone of your industry. Let manufacturing be developed, but agriculture must be fundamental. Brigham was most emphatic in discouraging the people fro running after gold or centering their thoughts and desires upon the riches of the world. His advice on this subject was fundamental. "Go to California, if you will, we will not curse you—we will not injure nor destroy, but we will pity you. If you must go for gold, and that is your God, go, and I promise you one thing: Every man that stays here and pays attention to his business will be able, within ten years, to buy out four of those who leave for the gold-ines."[9]

"Instead of hunting gold, let every man go to work at raising wheat, oats, barley, corn and vegetables, and fruit in abundance, that there may be plenty in the land. Raise sheep, and produce the finest quality of wool in large quantities. By the migratory system of feeding sheep in this country they will be healthy, and produce large clips of wool. I hope, by the blessings of the Lord, to demonstrate this the present season. In these pursuits are the true sources of wealth, and we have as much capital in these mountains to begin with as any people in the world, according to the number of our community. Real capital consists in knowledge and physical strength."[10]

This advice is good for this people today and always, for on it depends in the last analysis all economic success. Grain, not gold, is the basis of physical life, for people cannot eat money. A saying was coined in Germany during the difficult war period: "It is the farmer's wife that gets the egg." That is true today. The people of the world who will endure are those who are near to the earth—Mother Nature—and those who serve God.

The second principle may be simply stated: **People must work to be happy or successful.** That fact is most fundamental and will always be so. The Pioneers practiced it and their descendants must do so if they desire real success. Brigham was most emphatic in this; he had no patience with those who sat idly by, expecting others to care for them without any effort on their part. Yet he was most sympathetic to all those who were in distress or needed help in any way. He said on one occasion: "If we were to divide up our substance now equally amongst this people we would have to do it all over again in a year from now, for the thrifty and careful would have a surplus while the extravagant and shiftless would be without hope and in debt. For, you remember Bishop Hunter used to say there are the Lord's poor and the devil's poor and the poor devils, and we have all three kinds in this Church.

"My warfare is, and has been for years, to get the people to understand that if they do not take care of themselves they will not be taken care of; that if we do not lay the foundation to feed and clothe and shelter ourselves we shall perish with hunger and with cold; we might also suffer the summer season from the direct rays of the sun upon our naked and unprotected bodies."[11]

He was so insistent on the necessity of keeping people busy that he declared that if necessary people should build a wall and then tear it down again, rather than to be idle. For it is verily true, "an idle brain (or hand) is the devil's workshop."

The industries founded by Brigham Young and his associates were all of them profitable to those who undertook them as well as to those who received the benefits thereof. Labor of hand and brain, skilled or unskilled, was honored by Brigham Young, because he was himself a laborer. The industry which made Utah a busy hive of contented workmen, was blest of God and man. That instruction and promise given to Adam, "In the sweat of thy face shalt thou eat thy bread," was made glorious through knowledge of its profound meaning. The principles underlying these practices were necessary for the isolated peoples living a thousand miles from civilization. Had Brigham Young lived today, he would have understood the need for world concepts, rather than the isolation his people were forced to practice. The underlying principles would have guided him now as then.

As a commonwealth engineer, Brigham proved himself to be wise and just, and was unique in the zest and power which he inspired in his associates. They were mighty men and women.

CHAPTER 13

AS SOCIAL ENGINEER

THERE is a feeling abroad today that if one is to deal successfully with his fellow man, either as leader or teacher, one must be learned in the social sciences and have the proper background of academic experiences. The President of one of the modern churches told a friend recently that when he understood fully that he would one day be the leader of his sect he determined to educate himself in the social sciences. He therefore holds his Ph. D. degree in psychology, a graduate of one of the large universities of the country. This is undoubtedly fine preparation, but a leader of Christ's Church today as yesterday needs much more. He needs an absolute faith in God and His Son, and a direct commission from Him as a Leader; also that understanding which comes from a close communion with the Master of men and his Heavenly Father.

Webster defines sociology as "the science of the constitution, phenomena, and development of society." Comte is supposed to have founded the science in 1838. He defines it as "the science of the associated life of society."

It may be safely asserted that Brigham Young did not know or care for any such definition and would have felt the study of the subject in an academic sense to be a mere abstraction. Yet in spite of his opinion thereof and of his ignorance of the science, as such, he was undoubtedly one of the greatest sociologists of the past century, for he acted under the direct inspiration of a Higher Power. The society which he founded proves that statement.

Brigham's mastery of the subject leads one to ask: Where did he learn the technique of the arts and

sciences which he practiced? You will have to answer
that question. He tells naively some of his early preparation for life: "Brother Heber and I never went to school
until we got into Mormonism; that was the first of
our schooling. We never had the opportunity of letters
in our youth, but we had the privilege of picking up
brush, chopping down trees, rolling logs, and working
amongst the roots, and of getting our shins, feet, and
toes bruised. The uncle of brother Merril, who now sits
in the congegation, made me the first hat that my father
ever bought me; and I was then about eleven years of
age. I did not go bare headed previous to that time,
neither did I call on my father to buy me a five-dollar
hat every few months, as some of my boys do. My sisters would make me what was called a 'Jo-Johnson
cap' for winter, and in summer, I wore a straw hat
which I frequently braided for myself. I learned to make
bread, wash the dishes, milk the cows, and make butter; and I can make butter and beat most of the
women in this community at housekeeping. Those are
about all the advantages I gained in my youth. I know
how to economize for my father had to do it."[1] Yet that
he loved education and fostered it, is proven in a later
chapter. He said on another occasion:

"Among various other occupations I have been a
carpenter, painter and glazier, and when I learned my
trades and worked, both as journeyman and master, if
I took a job of painting and glazing, say to the amount
of one pound sterling, or five dollars, and through my
own carelessness injured the work or material, I considered it my duty to repair the injury at my own ex-
pense."[2]

Since experience is the best teacher, one may judge
that our pioneer ancestors learned their most valuable

lessons in the "School of Experience," being promoted therefrom into the "University of Hard Knocks." Yet their achievement was so mighty that their descendants marvel at their accomplishment.

A wise comment on the tremendous problems of the early colonization of the West was made by Mr. H. W. Laughy, managing editor of the San Gabriel Valley Courier, after a visit to the Bureau of Information on the Tabernacle grounds in Salt Lake City. "I said to your Doctor Young (Prof. Levi Edgar Young), a day or two back, in the museum at the Tabernacle, that I considered Moses a rank fourth-rater by comparison with your Brigham Young. Moses hid his followers, a people of a common ideal, in the wilderness apart from contamination, and there for a period of forty years preached to them submission to their God; yet we find the second generation of that same stock running hog-wild over the hill country of Canaan and licking the living daylights out of everything they could catch or corner.

"Brigham Young led a throng drawn from many nations, a people without a national tradition behind them, on a trek which stands without a precedent in human history. He sought no seclusion, faced contamination in a thousand forms, and beat down bare-handed every obstacle that came before him. He bowed the stiffest neck to meet the yoke, exalted the wild and wayward to the sublimity of humility, built tabernacles and temples to his God. Today, in his second and third generations [the sixth and seventh in fact], we find his covenants stamped upon the descendants of every singing pilgrim that marched behind him."

The settlement of the people of so many languages and countries in the valleys of this intermountain west, where they lived successful and happy lives of industry and contentment, is certainly the achievement of a master sociologist assisted as he was by stalwart men and women who were all sturdy God-fearing pioneers. All credit and honor to them!

Listen to this simple recital of experiences as told by Brigham Young: "We made and broke the road from Nauvoo to this place. Some of the time we ran by the compass; when we left the Missouri river we followed the Platte. And we killed rattlesnakes by the cord in some places; and made roads and built bridges till our backs ached. Where we could not build bridges across rivers, we ferried our people across, until we arrived here, where we found a few naked Indians, a few wolves and rabbits, and any amount of crickets; but as for a green tree or a fruit tree, or any green field, we found nothing of the kind, with the exception of a few cottonwoods and willows on the edge of City Creek. For some 1200 or 1300 miles we carried every particle of provision we had when we arrived here. When we left our homes we picked up what the mob did not steal of our horses, oxen and calves, and some women drove their own teams here. Instead of 365 pounds of breadstuff when they started from the Missouri river, there was not half of them had half of it. We had to bring our seed grain, our farming utensils, bureaus, secretaries, sideboards, sofas, pianos, large looking glasses, fine chairs, carpets, fire shovels and tongs, and other fine furniture, with all the parlor and cook stoves, etc., and we had to bring these things piled together with some women and children, helter skelter, topsy turvy, with broken down horses, ring-boned, spavined, pole evil, fistula and hipped; oxen with three legs and cows with one teat. This was our only means of transportation, and if we had not brought our goods in this manner we should not have had them, for there was nothing here. You may say this is a burlesque. Well, I mean it as such, for we, comparatively speaking, really came here naked and barefoot."[3]

"We are here in these mountains. Accidentally? Perhaps so. If we had Brother George A. Smith to tell the story, he would say we came here willingly because we were obliged to come, and we stay here because there is no other place to which we can go. We have built cities in this mountainous region, because there was no other place where we could do so. We have not got through with our work here yet. The people have hardly commenced to realize the beauty, excellence, and glory that will yet crown this city. I do not know that I will live in the flesh to see what I saw in vision when I came here. I see some things, but a great deal more has yet to be accomplished."[4]

It is evident that space forbids the treatment of but a tithe of the sociological experiences and experiments of the Pioneers. Brigham and the other leaders encouraged the people to practice all the arts of civilization. They fostered and built theatres, schools, universities, temples and churches, and the people prospered greatly because of their rich communal life.

The attempt to establish the United Order in the new country is a chapter of Mormon history that might be studied with profit today. Enoch knew God and taught his people (according to the revelations of Joseph Smith[5]) to hold earth possessions as a common property, and in this dedication to lose self in the good of the community. He was a consecrated prophet and leader and according to ancient and modern scripture was translated and did not taste death. The New Testament refers to the communal life of the early Christian

Church: "All that believed were together, and had all things common; and sold their possessions and goods, and parted them to all men, as every man had need."[6]

The rock upon which all such experiments split, and which will cause the failure today in Russia, in China, or wheresoever else such trials are made, is the inability of their leaders to recognize the fact that no unity of social and economic life can persist as a sociological experiment only. No economic-social unit may eradicate the seeds of selfishness weeded down in the soul of man. It is Christ alone who may give the supreme Magna Carta, and only His Spirit can drown out the ceaseless roar of selfishness as humans claim their rights. The love of Jesus cleanses the waters of doubt and washes away hatred and envy. May He hasten His coming in these days of ours!

Brigham was a devout believer in this Order revealed to the Prophet and felt that it was the most successful plan on earth for man's advancement. It was tried under his direction and met with great success in some instances; but even though it was a brave experiment, the leaders were forced to admit that the people generally were not yet prepared to usher in the the Order of Enoch. The experiment could scarcely be called a failure since it succeeded so admirably in a few instances. Those only who honor the law of tithing and other requirements of the Gospel of Christ may ever hope to live successfully the United Order. An attempt was made by many of the leaders who had large families to live by these principles.

Brigham Young's family life was exemplary in this respect. An interesting testimonial comes from Sister Manomus Andrus, a dear octogenarian of St. George, Utah. She states: "I worked for Aunt Zina Young; she was Zima Young Card's mother, and was a relative of my first husband. Brigham Young had the United Order in his home and it was nice, so peaceable and quiet and orderly. There was no quarreling and everything went smooth. Brigham Young was one of the kindest men in the world. I sat down at the table with them and the meals were lovely. The wives didn't have to do much work, just sewing and the like. It was at the White House and they had cooks and girls for everything. I did Aunt Zina's bedroom work and it was pleasant work."

The home life of this large family is of especial interest. Indeed it must have been unique where many mothers and children grew up in love and harmony that is seldom achieved in family relationships. And while the families did not always live together, yet the great majority of them lived in or near the Bee Hive and Lion Houses and on frequent occasions throughout the year the entire family was together.

That the unusual life in this family with many mothers may be understood, let one of the members of that family (my own dear mother, Susa Young Gates, who was the first child born in the Lion House) tell the story of this interesting home:

Plurality of wives is entirely Biblical and was permitted by our Heavenly Father in this dispensation solely for the purpose of giving mortal tabernacles through a worthy lineage to spirits who are waiting on the Other Side for that glorious privilege and who cannot advance until they are possessed of an earthly body and the experience of this mortal existence. Thus parenthood becomes a solemn privilege and thus that order of marriage was held as a religious sacrament to all those who lived it in righteousness. If undertaken merely for unworthy or physical reasons it would and did destroy those who practised it.

We were all as happy, mothers and children, as we could have been anywhere or under any other circumstances. Incredible as this sounds, the law of compensation, and the spirit or genius of the Lion House makes it true. Work and the mean pressure of grinding poverty was minimized and shared willingly by all. Above the whole of life bent an azure sky of divine conviction and conversion, lit by twinkling stars of human love, child to child, mother to mother, each conscious that God and our adored earthly father approved of us and shared our every joy and sorrow. His influence actually pervaded every corner of that Lion House and its vast surroundings. His love, we all knew, was as deep as that of our mothers, as understanding as was that of a bosom companion, and as surrounding as warmth and sunlight. On one occasion when he learned that one of his children was very ill and calling for him he stopped a council meeting declaring to the assembly that the meeting could wait, but his sick child could not.

His beautiful courtesy was never more in evidence than when he approached any one of his wives whom he loved and who loved him. Especially was that so when in the company of Mother Young, whose health was rather poor and who had borne the heat and burden of the day for him and with him. To her he paid exquisite attention, quiet, composed but sincere. His attitude and consideration were reflected in that of every other wife and child which he had.

The wives of Brigham Young lived together without outer friction or violent disagreement so far as any of us children knew. That they were all equally congenial could not be expected for they were not weaklings and all "had minds of their own." But their differences, if and when they existed, were their own affairs and were settled amongst themselves without disturbing in the slightest degree the serene tranquillity of our family life. They were ladies, and lived their lives as such. The children were never aware of any quarrels and indeed they could not have been serious or the children must have been aware of them.

The joy, the happiness of their lives came through the delightful upspringing growth in spiritual beauty, in the confidence and friendship of each other, and in the reverence and love manifested by their intelligent God-fearing husband, Brigham

Young who knew the difficult upward path they each were treading because of the strain which justice and mercy put upon him in the adjustments and readjustments necessary for himself.

The world knows Brigham Young as a statesman and colonizer; but to his children he was an ideal father. Kind to a fault, tender, thoughtful, just and firm. He spoke but once, and none were so daring as to disobey. That his memory is almost worshipped by all who bear his name is an eloquent tribute to his character. None of us feared him; all of us adored him. If the measure of a man's greatness is truly given by Carlyle, as bounded by the number of those who love him and who were loved by him, then few men are as great as was my father, Brigham Young. What his life and love meant to his family only their subsequent lives may testify. What he did as State-founder, Commonwealth builder, only the pages of history may imperfectly recall.

The foregoing statement of authenticated fact is in no sense an advocacy of present day plural marriage for today sees the Mormon Church as faithfully committed to the monogamic form of marriage, as it was to another form in past years.[7]

A more intimate personal picture is given by the Leader himself: "I will relate a little of my course and experience in my family. I have a large family of children, many of them small, and yet I do not think that you ever saw even four children in one family live together with so little contention. Watch them, and their conduct will prove that there is a good spirit influencing them. I never knew one of them to be accidentally hurt, without more sympathy being extended to that one than the whole of them needed. You may ask how I manage to bring this result. I seldom give a child a cross word; I seldom give a wife a cross word; and I tell my wives never to give a child cause to doubt their word."[8]

How many parents today could say as much?

The wisdom of the social doctrines of Brigham Young is evident. He taught principles that must be

applied today and always if human beings are to enjoy even a semblance of social or economic equality:
"Take any community, three-eights of whom are living
on the labor of the remaining five-eights, and you find
the few are living on the many. Take the whole world,
and comparatively few of its inhabitants are producers.
If the members of this community wish to get rich and
to enjoy the fruits of the earth, they must be producers
as well as consumers."[9]

"You take some of those characters to whom I have
referred today, who want us all to be of one heart and
of one mind, and they think we cannot be so unless we
all have the same number of houses, farms, carriages,
and horses, and the same amount in greenbacks. There
are plenty in this Church who entertain such a notion,
and I do not say but there are good men who, if they
had the power, would dictate in this manner, and in
doing so they would exercise all the judgment they are
masters of. But let such characters guide and dictate,
and they would soon accomplish the overthrow of this
Church and people. This is not what the Lord meant
when He said: 'Be ye of one heart and of one mind.'
He meant that we must be one in observing His word
and in carrying out His counsel, and not to divide our
worldly substance so that a temporary equality might
be made among the rich and the poor."

"I recollect once the people wanted to sell their
jewelry to help the poor; I told them that would not
help them. The people wanted to sell such things so
that they might be able to bring into camp three, ten,
or a hundred bushels of corn meal. Then they would
sit down and eat it up, and would have nothing with
which to buy another hundred bushels of meal, and
would be just where they started. My advice was for

them to keep their jewelry and valuables, and to set the poor to work—settting out orchards, splitting rails, digging ditches, making fences, or anything useful, and so enable them to buy meal and flour and the necessaries of life."[10]

The necessity of wise recreation in the daily life of everyone was taught and practiced by the Pioneers— otherwise their task had been well-nigh impossible. No one understood this better than Brigham Young, and through his wise grasp of the needs of the people, ample provision for wholesome amusements was made. The best music was encouraged, as well as dancing, drama, and even operas and oratories were presented most creditably.

The response of the people was wholesome and a measurable degree of culture was the result. Mr. Tullidge speaks thus of this procedure. "It is well known to those who have studied even casually the character of that wonderful Mormon society-founder, Brigham Young, that he supplied his people with the agencies of both social and physical revivification. Not to say it flippantly, but with a simple appreciation of his unique character, had Brigham Young been the leader of ancient Israel as he was of modern Israel, and typified with his Vermont sagacity, there would have been no rebellion of the congregation in the wilderness and no repining for the flesh-pots of Egypt. This was strikingly exemplified in the great 'Mormon' exodus to the mountains; he constantly vivified the people whom he led by enlivening instrumental music, by the singing of familiar songs of home in the spirit of home present and not far away, in the merry dance, social ball. Like the ark of a new covenant, the people under his leader-

ship carried with them on their long and tedious journey
to the Rocky Mountains at least a primitive civilization.

"Capt. Pitt and his band left Nauvoo on the same
day with Brigham Young, February 15, 1846, crossing
the Mississippi on the ice and with him journeyed that
day to the 'Camp of Israel' which waited for the leader on
'Sugar Creek.' At night the weather was bitterly cold
but the trumpet by the order of Brigham called the
camp out to a concert in the open air, and the Nauvoo
Brass Band performed its best selections, after which the
pilgrims joined in the dance and the music was as joyous
as at a merrymaking. In the Valley, the dance to the
Mormons became almost an institution and the ball as
a social sacrament."[11]

**The stake quarterly and general semi-annual confer-
ences** of the Church were instituted to bring the people
together at regular intervals in religious and social con-
tacts. It is difficult to estimate the value of this social
and religious stimulus on the lives of the people. Brigham realized this and often made occasions at intervals
other than at the regular conferences to meet the people
in their home towns, when times of general rejoicing
were enjoyed. One such journey is described by Brother
Isaiah M. Coombs, one of the leading pioneer teachers
of Payson, Utah.

This interesting first-hand picture was taken from
his diary by his daughter, Mrs. Ida Coombs Lund:

Thursday, Sept. 17, 1868. Taught school today, and dismissed school this evening until Monday as Prest. Brigham Young
is expected here tomorrow. He is at Provo tonight.

Friday, 18. The Sabbath School convened at the Hall at 4
o'clock P. M. where we formed a procession at 5 o'clock and
marched out to the east end of Main Street to receive Prest.
Young and company. Our school presented a very beautiful ap-

pearance being drawn up in two lines with beautiful banners bearing appropriate mottos. At 7 o'clock there was a meeting at the Hall and preaching by Brothers J. W. Young, Dunford, T. Taylor and the President. He shook hands with me and inquired very kindly after my affairs and family.

Sept. 19. At 8 A. M. a number of us assembled at the Hall by invitation of the Prest. and were there organized into a School of the Prophets with Bp. J. B. Fairbanks of Payson as Prest., Bp. Thurber of Spanish Fork as Vice Prest. and myself as Secy., Orawell Simons as Treas. The rules, 17 in number, were read and sustained. The Prest. made a few remarks in relation to the school which is to teach the Elders the principles of government and how to build up the Zion of God on the earth. As soon as school was dismissed the Prest. and company stepped into their carriages and drove on their journey south. Soon after I started after them in company with two others in a carriage hired for the trip. Arrived in Santaquin for meeting; tarried there for dinner and we rolled out as soon as meeting was dismissed. Made a halt at Mona until the Prest. came up when we fell into the rear and rolled on to Nephi. We were received with open arms. About six miles from town we were met with a body of cavalry who escorted us to town. Further we met a lot of mounted men and boys and in the suburbs of town the brass band was stationed who conducted us under a splendid triumphal arch with the motto "Zion's Chieftain Ever Welcome."

The Sunday School and citizens were out in force arranged in a long line on the side walk to receive the Prest. Not the least attractive portion of the assembly was 24 young ladies dressed in white. Brother H. Goldsbrough invited me to make my stay at his home. After the supper, went to meeting and was invited to the stand and opened the meeting with prayer. Preaching was by Bros. Van Cott, Jos. W. Young, Jos. F. Smith and A. M. Musser. We were just 4 hours in making the trip today 20 miles.

Sunday 20. I attended Sunday School where we were addressed by Wilford Woodruff, Jos. F. Smith and Geo. Q. Cannon. The school numbered over 300 pupils. After another good meeting, a Private Council was held at the schoolhouse at which the Prest. invited me to join them. At this Council a Stake Organization was effected, also a School of the Prophets. The

object of all the teaching was to unite the people together that
we may be prepared to sustain ourselves and the kingdom.
Telegraphed my wife that I could not be home until Tuesday.
Never enjoyed meetings better. They were wonderful! glorious!

That Brigham Young had faults no one will deny,
for being human, he must have had his own character
struggles to become the great leader he was. No attempt
is here made to glamorize him or make him appear to be
greater than he was. One day his daughter Susa said to
him, "Father I wish I were as good a woman as you are
a man and that I was as sure of salvation as you are."
He looked at her understandingly and replied: "Don't
think for a moment, daughter, that my upward climb is
any easier than yours. My struggle to keep Brigham on
the path of righteousness is just as difficult as is yours."
At another time he said that he was fully conscious of
his mistakes, but his enemies were so busy mag-
nifying them that he could only hope his friends
would be more charitable. "Yet he said little about his
faults, or about other's faults. Once he rebuked his
daughter for relating in detail one of her own character
weaknesses. 'Don't do that,' he said. 'If you were holding a fort against an enemy, you wouldn't get up in a
gap in the wall and shout, "Here is a hole, climb in
here!" He said again: "Confess your faults to the individuals you ought to confess them to, and proclaim
them not on the house tops. Be careful that you wrong
not yourselves. If persons lose confidence in themselves,
it takes away the strength, faith and confidence that
others have in them. If you committed sin that no other
person on earth knows of, and which harms no other
one, you have done a wrong and you have sinned against
your God, but keep that within your own bosom, and
seek to God and confess there, and get pardon for your

sin—confess your sins to whomsoever you have sinned against and let it stop there.

"What perfect psychology he had, taught by the Master of men's minds![12]

A love of home and the land which gives sustenance was deeply inculcated in the sociological principles fostered by the Pioneers. As a result the people of this State today are amongst those who have the highest percentage of home owners of any people in the world. **The Country Gentleman** for January 29, 1921, page 12, says: "Utah should be called the home-owner State. Out of 25,662 farms in Utah, seven-eights of them are operated by the owners." This must always be a chief guiding principle for this people if they would endure.

As a natural sociologist and leader of men Brigham Young stands pre-eminent.

CHAPTER 14.

AS EDUCATIONAL LEADER

IT is noteworthy that the men chosen by the Lord to usher in the new dispensation, like those chosen by our Savior, were in the main unlettered men with little or no book-learning or formal education. Does this fact indicate that men who are unlearned in worldly knowledge are more susceptible to spiritual guidance? Undoubtedly it may be a warning to those who seek the learning of the world that they must keep themselves "lowly in spirit" and near to God if they would be well rounded spiritually and morally as well as mentally. Certain it is that if a man thinks "he knows it all' or that the learning of the world is all-sufficient, there is little room in his thoughts or life for the guidance of his Heavenly Father.

The Prophet who ushered in this dispensation, as well as his successor Brigham Young and most of the moving hosts of modern Israel, were untutored in worldly learning, yet how resourceful they were because of their very dependence on an over-ruling Power. However, Brigham well knew and taught that man to be fully prepared must have the learning of the world, all he can get and use, but with it must keep himself near to his Father in Heaven.

Brigham Young's definition of education is one well worth remembering: "Education is the power to think clearly, the power to act well in the world's work, and the power to appreciate life." No learned man could devise a better one, and an ignorant man could not have thought it out or expressed it so tersely yet comprehensively.

The Pioneers loved education and all that it stood for. Even while crossing the plains, whenever the moving camps halted for a day or more, the precious school books and slates were brought out of safe packing and children were grouped around their appointed teachers to "learn their letters and to do their sums." Even during the very first long winter in the Valley, schools were held in the rudely constructed Fort where the people lived for protection against the Indians. The children were taught by a fine cultured lady, Mary Dilworth; and another school for older people was conducted by Burr Frost. This would be expected from a people who teach that "The glory of God is Intelligence." These primitive schools were the first of the very superior system of education existing in our State today.

The founding of a University in the year 1850, only three short years after the entrance of the people into a wild and desert country, is a fact of which all Utahns may feel justly proud. It bespeaks a people who loved and fostered education as a necessary adjunct to life. Our University thus becomes the oldest State University of the West.

In his message to the Legislature as Governor of the Territory, in 1852, Brigham says: "In nearly all the different districts good school houses are, or are being erected, and great attention is being paid to common schools. There are also many languages and various accomplishments of music, etc. A Mathematical School is much needed, and it is most sincerely hoped that such a course will be adopted in relation to it, that one will be established upon a permanent basis. I cannot too earnestly recommend to your favorable consideration, this subject, fraught as it is, with the deepest interest to the well being of the rising generation, which will, ere long, be our representatives upon the earth."

As a matter of survey he said: "I give it as my opinion that you may go to any part of the United States or of the world, where parents are not obliged by law to send their children to school, and you will find more schools in the midst of this people, notwithstanding their poverty, their drivings, sufferings, and persecutions, and more persons that can read and write in proportion to our population, than in any other place on this earth. You may select any community of the same number, and in this particular we will favorably compare with the best of them, and I think we are ahead of them. But this furnishes us no reason for keeping children from school. There are many who are anxious to teach school, if the people will encourage them. The people have the privilege of sending their children to school for there are plenty of teachers and plenty of rooms in every town and neighborhood."[1]

The refusal of the central government to give the aid to education in Utah that had been given to other territoies was greatly deplored by him. Said he: "We have no societies or persons to assist us in our efforts to school ourselves and our children; we never have had, and the feeling that is now exhibited, and which has always been shown towards us since the organization of the kingdom of God upon the earth, is that those who are our enemies would rather spend ten, yea, a hundred dollars to deprive us of the least privilege in the world, than give us one cent towards schooling our children.

"Has the government given us the privilege of one acre of land to educate our children here? No. The school land is kept from us, and we get no benefit therefrom."[2]

Yet from the first, schools were organized and the people encouraged to send their children, both young and older ones. Brigham's disapproval of men who would not sacrifice to keep their children in school knew no bounds. On one occasion he said: "Some say they are not able to send their children to school. In such case, I think I would rise in the morning, wash myself, take a little 'composition' [herb tea] and try, if possible, to muster strength enough to send my children to school, and pay their tuition like a man. When you have done this, if you are still unable, apply to some of your neighbors to assist you.

"Men able to ride in their carriages, and not able or willing to pay their children's tuition, ought, I think, to have a little catnip tea; and then perhaps, they will be able to send their children to school! I know such persons are weak and feeble; but the disease is in the brain and heart—not in the bones, flesh, and blood. Send your children to school."[3]

The cause of co-education had hearty support from him, as proved by the fact that all common schools and the newly founded University of Deseret were for girls and women as well as for boys and men. Thus the University of Utah was one of the first co-educational institutions in the United States. On this subject he said at one time: "Brother Calder commences tomorrow to teach our youth and those of middle age the art of bookkeeping and impart to them a good mercantile education. We expect soon to have our sisters join in the class and mingle with the brethren in their studies for why should not a lady be capable of taking charge of her husband's business affairs when he goes into the grave? We have sisters now engaged in several of our telegraph offices, and we wish them to learn not only to act as operators but to keep the books of our offices, and let sturdy men go to work at some employment for which by their strength they are adapted, and we hope eventually to see every store in Zion attended by ladies. We wish to have our young boys and girls taught in the different branches of an English education, and in other languages, and in the various sciences, all of which we intend eventually to have taught in this school."[4]

Brigham's attitude to women and their work was fair and enlightened. No "inferiority complex" is possible for women in this church unless they prove themselves inferior. Their free agency to act for themselves as individuals was recognized from the organization of the Church. That Brigham Young sensed their power may be drawn from so many of his words and deeds.

In talking to the Relief Society on one occasion he said: "Here are mothers. Who gives the key to the nations of the earth with regard to their feelings, pride, prejudices; their religion, habits, customs, and, I may say, who in a great degree governs the nations because they lay the foundations for the ability that is exhibited among men? It is the mothers. Who have laid the foundations in the hearts of the children to prepare them to be great and good men? **It is not the fathers—it is the mothers.** It is like the saying of the Savior with regard to the poor. Speaking to his disciples he says, "For the poor always ye have with you, but me ye have not always." Now the children are always with the mother, and the mother is always with the children, but the father they have not. He is in the field, at his work; and the mother is all the time making impressions upon the minds of the children. . . .

"You mothers, are the moving instrument in the hand of Providence to guide the destinies of nations; teach your children not to make war but to be peace-makers. . . . "[5]

Again on one occasion he said: "Every man or woman that has talent and hides it will be called a slothful servant. * * * Go to school and study; have the girls go, and teach them chemistry, so that they can take any of these rocks and analyze them. The sciences can be learned without much difficulty. I want to have schools to entertain the minds of the people, and draw them out to learn all the arts and sciences."[6]

His personal efforts to improve himself are encouraging to all. He tells of an amusing incident which proves this and also shows how, even in youth, he was careful of his diet: "I recollect what was said to me in my youth by a journeyman printer. We were working off Ball's arithmetic together and we boarded together. I did not eat meat at that time, and he was very fond of it. We went into the office one day from dinner and he said to the workmen, 'Young never eats meat.' I said to him, 'Mr. Pratt, if you will step here into the middle of the floor, I will show you how to dirty coats.' But he dared not try it. They say ladies do not eat enough to make them strong—why I have seen scores and scores of them that could pull a hand press."[7]

Though, as he said, he had but eleven days formal schooling in his life. He may be called a truly self-educated and well educated man. An incident showing his method of improving his vocabulary is told by his daughter Susa. One day her father asked her to look up the definition of a certain word. She did so and repeated it to him. "Write it down on a piece of paper," said he. He took it, re-read it, then folded the paper and placed it in his silver spectacle case. The next Sunday she heard him in a sermon speak of the autonomy of Russia. The word she had looked up for him was "autonomy." He had made the word his own.

The need of moral and religious education was deeply sensed by this able pioneer. He was a firm believer
in the separation of church and state, and was averse
to religious education being a part of the state school
curriculum. Yet he could forsee what kind of men and
women would develop from a schooling which educated
mind and body only leaving the soul and spirit to be
given haphazard development or none at all. He sensed
deeply that to be fully educated one must be trained
to use aright the body, the heart, and the soul, as well
as the mind.

For that reason when it became evident that the
youth of his people were sensing the absence of such
training in the public schools he undertook to devise
ways and means of establishing Church schools in all
the more populous districts, which were to be followed
with institutions of higher learning.

Brigham Young Academy (now University) was
founded by him in October, 1875, with every provision
for a well rounded academic curriculum, but in addition it was to teach such subjects as would develop the
hand as well as the head, and especially it was to form
the character of students, as well as to give them a
knowledge of the Gospel of Jesus Christ. Said he in his
instructions to the first principal, "Brother Maeser, do
not teach even the multiplication tables without the
spirit of the Lord to accompany you. Let it direct the
spirit of all your teaching and everything that is done
in the school." Those instructions have been followed
from that time to the present.

Brigham Young College at Logan was founded in
July, 1877, and was endowed by him with "certain real
property," as stated in its articles of incorporation. Its
scope was similar to that of the Brigham Young Uni-

versity, and its purpose exactly the same. The school was in operation for nearly fifty years and the good it accomplished for the youth of its day is incalculable.

As a pioneer in vocational and industrial education Brigham Young is unique. One of his cherished ideals in founding the Brigham Young Academy and the Brigham Young College was that the youth of Israel might learn how to employ their hands in useful labor. The deed of trust of both schools state specifically: "The students who shall take full courses shall be taught, if their physical ability will permit, some useful branch of mechanism that shall be suited to their taste and capacity." In order to prove his understanding of the fundamental nature of industrial education the following quotation is given. This also answers the slanders of enemies that the Mormons are "an ignorant lot."

"It is said by our enemies that the Latter-day Saints are an ignorant people. I ask all the nations of Christendom if they can produce a people, considering all the circumstances, who are better educated in all the great branches of learning than this people, as a people? Many of them have been brought from poverty, and have been placed in comfortable circumstances in these mountains, where they have been taught how to get their living from the elements, and to become partially self-sustaining. How much do you know among the nations? Can you make an axe helve? 'Yes,' and so can we, and make an axe to fit it, and then we know how to use it. We can make a hoe-handle and a hoe to fit it, and then we know how to hoe the ground with it. Can we make a plough? Yes, and know how to use it as well as any people on the earth. We can make every agricultural implement, and can use it. We can make a cambric needle; and we can make the steam engine and vessel to carry it. We can direct the lightning, and make it our servant, after Franklin showed us how; and the philosophers of the day are as dependent on his discoveries as we are. We have all the improvements that have been made in the arts and sciences, and know how to use them to our advantage. We can make boots and shoes for the sturdy, plodding agriculturist in the field, and for the delicate lady in the parlor, and we know how to make the leather as well as others do.

"We can read the Bible and understand it, and our lexicographers can make dictionaries. Wherein, then, are we more ignorant than others? We have good mechanics, good philosophers, good astronomers, good mathematicians, good architects, good theologians, good historians, good orators, good statesmen, good school teachers, and we can make a good prayer and preach a good sermon. We know how to make cloth, how to make it into garments, and wear it; we know how to provide for ourselves, how to protect ourselves, and ask nobody to help us but God our Heavenly Father. Then, wherein are we so woefully ignorant as some people make us out to be? We know how to build houses, and can make the furniture to furnish them; we know how to plant gardens, set out orchards, and plant vineyards. We know how to raise all kinds of vegetables, fruit, and grain, and everything else that will flourish in this altitude. Wherein are we ignorant? We know and read history; we understand the geography of the world, the manners, customs, and laws of nations. Our astronomers describe to us the geography of the heavens, measure the distance between the earth and the sun, moon and planets. We have learned to speculate on all these works of God, and revelations unfolding reliable knowledge on many of the wonders of the heavens.

"Now, wherein are we more ignorant than other people? Is it because we believe the Bible, which declares that man is made in the likeness and image of God, that He has ears to hear our prayers, eyes to see His handiwork, a stretched-out arm to defend His people, and to make bare to punish the wicked nations of the earth? Wherein are we ignorant? We understand the laws of domestic and civil government; we know how to conduct ourselves like men of sense, like gentlemen and Christians; we understand natural philosophy and medicine; and are satisfied of the emptiness of the vain philosophy of the world. If believing and knowing what we do constitute ignorance, then let us be ignorant still, and continue in the way which will lead us to the perfection of knowledge which the world calls ignorance."[8]

With this choice elucidation of learning or true education in mind, Brigham Young may be considered a man who understood education, though he were untrained in college, and could not boast a college degree. Yet in all his teaching there is a strong urge for the young people of his time and all time to avail themselves of all possible educational advantages of school and college, but they must add thereto a knowledge of God and the wisdom that comes from on High. This combination of learning makes one truly educated and happy no matter what one's outward circumstances may be; for one who is truly educated may control circumstances for the richer, fuller life of the sprit as well as of the mind and body.[9]

A pioneer agricultural experiment station was indicated by these early state builders. Their foresight in fostering new enterprises is most commendable and re-markable in many ways. The founding of the cotton in-dustry had just begun in Utah's "Dixie" and was meet-ing with some difficulty. No such thing as State Ex-periment Stations had been dreamed of in those early days; in fact, the first agricultural experiment station in the world had been founded privately in England less than a decade before. Yet here in the desert just such an undertaking was begun and made a matter of legisla-tive enactment.

In one of the early sessions of the territorial legisla-ture was created a Council Committee on Agriculture, Trade, and Manufactures, which functioned to the great advantage of industries in those early days. Brigham Young himself set up the first machinery to tabulate irrigation and manufacturing experiments. He appointed his counselor, George A. Smith, as Chairman of the Committee.

The report of this committee is most interesting: "Your committee are of opinion that the appropriation of a small sum to be expended for premiums would in-duce experiments on different kinds of soil, modes of watering, and culture, and cause a knowledge of the management of the cotton crop to become more gen-erally diffused, by which means many obstacles to the cultivation of cotton would be overcome, and our moun-tain home be made to produce the necessary articles in sufficient quantities, and on such reasonable terms, as to insure successful competition with the imported ar-ticle.

"We therefore beg leave to report the annexed.

"George A. Smith.

"Chairman of Council Committee on Agriculture, Trade, and Manufactures, Great Salt Lake City, December 27, 1859."

In the sense of being prepared to meet life's problems successfully Brigham Young was a highly educated man. Life and his Father in Heaven were his teachers. He was always an apt and industrious student. He led himself and others to daily improvement of mind and heart and thus became a real educational expert.

That the People of Utah have continued to practice the advice given by these stalwart pioneer leaders is proven by their educational record from that day to this. In school attendance at all age levels, Utah far exceeds every other state as well as in the number of high school and college graduates.

"Utah leads all of the states of the union in the number of scientific men born there in proportion to the population, it is revealed by an analysis of **American Men of Science.**" This assertion was made by Science News Letter, August 31, 1940, and is based upon research of Dr. Edward L. Thorndike, emeritus professor of educational psychology, Teachers College, Columbia University, who surveyed American scientists for the Carnegie Foundation, classifying them according to the state of their origin.

"As reported by Dr. E. L. Thorndike of Columbia University, the number of scientists born in Utah per million population for the period 1870 to 1900, as listed in the 1938 edition of 'American Men of Science,' represents a lead of thirty per cent over the next highest state and is double the national average. Further corroborative evidence appears in the Scientific Monthly for May 1943 in an article by Professor Thorndike called 'The Origin of Superior Men.' "[9]

Education is loved and fostered by the people of Utah as proven by their record.

CHAPTER 15.

BRIGHAM YOUNG AS STATESMAN

IT IS impossible for people to prosper and live in happy communities without the existence of wise and just laws administered for the protection and benefit of every individual in the community. Each man must be protected in his own rights, but these rights may never infringe upon the rights of others. So have lived the Mormons, always.

Government during the first two years in the Valley was entirely ecclesiastic, since there was no need for civil authority. All difficulties which arose were settled by the Bishop's Court or High Council of the Church. Later, as the influx of the California emigrants brought foreign elements into the settlements, a distinct body of civil laws was found to be practical and necessary.

A general political convention was called in March, 1849 to meet in Great Salt Lake City. All people anywhere in the Great Basin or beyond, from Oregon to the Pacific, were invited to participate. The "Provisional State of Deseret" (which was to include practically the entire basin of the Colorado river) was formed, and a constitution was adopted. Brigham Young as Governor and other officers were duly elected.

Meanwhile the people had sent petition after petition to the central Government at Washington that they be admitted into the Union with state or territorial status. Finally these petitions were acted upon and in September, 1850, a bill designating the Territory of Utah was passed by Congress. Federal and local officers were duly appointed and through the influence of a loyal and true friend, Thomas L. Kane, Brigham Young was appointed Governor by the President of the United States.

In the civil administration of Brigham Young he proved himself to be a wise and prudent official with a grasp of public affairs which places him in the class of truly great statesmen. His Messages to the Legislature express the simple, comprehensive recommendations of a practical idealist. They might well have been delivered by Governor Winthrop to the struggling colony of Massachusetts' Puritans in 1640. The message of 1852 which is here quoted throws a torch light on his views of law and laws, of education and of economics. His words on the folly of having statute books crowded with dead-letter laws are even more applicable to present conditions than to those primitive times. His advice to the people to acquaint themselves with the laws, each man becoming his own lawyer, is sound and vital to good government.

His broad outlook on economic factors in state-building was crystalized into the prosperity and stability which have marked the growth of this commonwealth. No saner views of broad economic principles have ever been expressed by any leader or student of the science of economics, even to the present time, than are expressed in these wonderful state documents. They epitomize much that is known today in this important field of science.

Just treatment of the surrounding tribes of Indians, road building, irrigation needs, bridges, public buildings and improvements are all carefully considered. Iron production is recommended; beet-sugar raising is advocated with the added information, startling for that early day and pioneer place, that both beet-seed machinery and skilled workmen had been brought over from Europe for this purpose. Wollen, leather and crockery manufacture is noted as already in successful operation. While, more wonderful still, this advocate of economic independence advises men to gather forces and equipment for the making of machinery which shall manufacture the machinery itself.

If Brigham had been familiar with Thomas Jeffersons' address he could not have more plainly set forth Jefferson's own ideas concerning the evils of urban life. Said Jefferson: "The general desire of men to live by their heads rather than their hands, and the strong allurements of great cities to those who have any turn for dissipation, threaten to make them here as in Europe, sink-holes of voluntary misery." Brigham Young urged the people to plow and cultivate their farms, establish industries of all kinds, and to find their pleasure in the midst of their families and homes.

There are many documents to prove the above statements. In the one here quoted, the cause of education is held paramount. University buildings and appropriations are held as necessities of intelligent citizenship. Ignorance and idleness are two destructive forces of organized society as understood by the Leader and his associates. Naturally, co-education is implied as it was understood and practiced in Kirtland and in Nauvoo.

The Message is a glimpse into the past, the then present, and the future life and destiny of its author and the Territory of which he was the representative.

This Message to the Legislature (December 13, 1852), which is one of many equally as wise and far-seeing, is too long to give here but its contents are most interesting. Following are a few brief quotations:

To the Members of the Council, and House of
   Representatives of the Legislature of Utah.

Gentlemen:

Through the manifold blessings of an indulgent God, we are met to again consider the public interest, and to adopt such rules, regulations, and measures as shall best subserve the welfare of the people, and promote the weal of the rising state.

Our most profound acknowledgements are due to the Giver of all good, who hath caused the earth to bring forth in it strength, the grains and the rich fruits thereof; and crowned the efforts of the passing year with an abundant harvest.

We are cheered by the glad sounds of peace and prosperity which reach us from all parts of the Territory. No sound of war has awakened the lonely dell or disturbed the unbroken quiet of the peaceful settlements, indicating a peaceful disposition on the part of our tawney neighbors, hitherto unknown.

Many hostile bands of the native tribes, have smoked the pipe of peace and renewed friendly relations which long before had ceased to exist, which the exercise of a genial influence, by the rapidly extending settlements of the whites, is believed may be strengthened, and it is hoped will be enduring.

A proper consideration in the formation of laws, is calculated to prevent litigation. Laws suitable to the situation and circumstances of the people, who are to be affected by them, and for the uniform rule of practice and decision of the courts throughout the Territory, are desirable and necessary. It should moreover be the aim of the law-making departments, to study simplicity in their enactments, that every person may approach the Temple of Justice, either in his own defense, or to obtain that justice which should without unnecessary delay be impartially administered to all, whether rich or poor, bond or free, black or white. Let every man, if he choose, be his own lawyer, and never invest your courts with mists and fogs, or the mirage, if you please, of bygone ages; as we find to be too frequently the case, as though there had been made no advancement in the science of law, as well as the other learned professions.

Domestic manufacturers, I am happy to state, are in a flourishing condition, considerable quantities of leather and crockery having found their way into market, and a large amount of clothing has been made, principally by the hands of the "Good Housewife," who thereby adds dignity to her station, and reflects credit and honor upon her household. Specimens of iron have also been forwarded from the works in Iron County, which, for the first run, were exceedingly flattering.

A liberal hand should be extended unto the enterprising men who have nobly devoted their time, under circumstances of penury and want, in producing an article of so much moment as iron, to the urgent necessities, and future wealth of the territory. It will soon pay its own way, and become a source of profit to the producers; but until returns can be received, the enterprise exhausts the means of operators, and they should be relieved by the public funds.

Then follows in the Message instructions as to the encouragement of woolen manufacture, of the beginnings of the beet-sugar industry, of the extension and enlargement of irrigation canals and ditches, and every species of domestic manufacture. Instructions regarding a University for higher learning are emphatic with deep regret expressed that funds did not permit its immediate construction. The military interests of the community are stressed for protection only, while on the subject of home manufacture the Message is eloquent with good advice:

Unquestionably, in a sparsely peopled country, settled by those persons, who have exhausted all their means in accomplishing their journey, manufactures must spring up in the domicile of the citizen, the spinning wheel and the hand-loom must discourse their parlor music, and chant melodies at the fireside of the thrifty artizan. A thousand miles land transportation will long afford protection and encouragement for such productions. The territory is fast filling up with the requisite material; and a growing disposition on the part of the people, to furnish their own supplies—to rely upon their own exertions and home productions for home consumption, will surely result in ample resources of wealth and independence to the people, and add dignity and influence to the state. The road to affluence is not pursued by any surer method, than by a well directed industry and perseverence. Labor is wealth, and supplies the world with luxuries, comforts, and necessaries, which gold could never purchase. The former is productive of wealth, but the latter impoverishes. In the poverty of the state, but little if any direct assistance can be granted; but sanctioned by law, may greatly tend to inspire enterprise. I do therefore most earnestly desire, that you will lend your aid, influence, and power, to promote the cause of home manufactures. It will also have a tendency to classify labor, and create a market for the products of the soil.

Especially should this be noted: "It is better to have no law, and so understood by the people than one, no matter how wise in its provision, yet to remain as a dead letter upon the statute book."

The affairs of local government are reviewed and the lack of national support deplored.

"It is gratifying to behold in the people of the Territory, an inflexible determination to progress in public enterprise and improvements; **notwithstanding the neglect of Congress,** in affording them those facilities always accorded to other Territories. It will not prove detrimental to the energies, the enterprise, and the general well being of the community, to be thus thrown upon their own resources, and compelled to progress through poverty in funds, by their united labors, and untiring exertions (which in reality constitute true wealth) to that station in society, which knowing no friends, fears no enemies. To Congress, it is poor policy, and a burning disgrace. To Utah, a present blessing, and a future benefit which their hoarded coffers can never equal.

Then let us struggle on, and being taught in the school of adversity, we shall be the better prepared to appreciate, and enjoy anticipatory blessings, which will be sought, and surely obtained through self-exertion, and the rightly directed industry and enterprise of the people.

This is but one of many scholarly, far-reaching documents presented by Brigham Young which prove him to be a statesman as well as a loyal patriot.

The story of Johnston's Army in Utah is one of the most thrilling in history. No people were ever more loyal to their government than the persecuted people who had been forced to leave their homes again and again and finally to wander into an unchartered West.

Yet because of the lies and slander of corrupt Eastern federal officials who hated the people and misrepresented them in Washington, an army was sent in early 1857 to settle a supposed rebellion that never existed. It would be interesting to review the events of "Buchanan's Blunder," as it has been called, did time and space permit. The people vowed that never again would they leave their homes untouched for their enemies as they had done in Kirtland, Ohio, in Jackson County, Missouri, and in Nauvoo, Illinois. If they were to be driven again, they would burn their homes and gardens and leave a barren desert for their enemies. This they prepared to do when they were forced to admit the army. As a body the people moved south to Provo and surrounding country leaving guards behind to "fire" their homes if the army attempted to inhabit them.[1]

The opinion of an outside observer is particularly interesting. We quote an extract from the **New York Times** of that period regarding the "move south":

Whatever our opinion may be of "Mormon" morals or "Mormon" manners, there can be no question that this voluntary and even cheerful abandonment by 40,000 people of homes created by wonderful industry, in the midst of trackless wastes, after years of hardship and persecution, is something from which no one who has a particle of sympathy with pluck, fortitude, and constancy can withhold his admiration. Right or wrong, sincerity thus attested is not a thing to be sneered at. True or false, a faith to which so many men and women prove their loyalty, by such sacrifices, is a force in the world. After this last demonstration of what fanaticism can do, we think it would be most unwise to treat Mormonism as a nuisance to be abated by a **posse comitatus.** It no is longer a social excrescence to be cut off by the sword; it is a power to be combatted by the most skillful, political, and moral treatment. When people abandon their homes to plunge with women and children into a wilderness, to seek new settlements, they know not where, they give a higher proof of

courage than if they fought for them. When the Dutch submerged
Holland, to save it from invaders, they had heartier plaudits show-
ered on them than if they had fertilized its soil with their blood.
We have certainly the satisfaction of knowing that we have to
deal with foemen worthy of our steel. In fact, the whole military
movement against them seems to have been a blunder, and to
have accomplished nothing.[2]

As is well-known, the army did not remain here
long, for they were soon thereafter called east to enter
a real rebellion brewing between the North and the
South.

Brigham's conduct of affairs of state while he acted
as Governor and afterward was exemplary. During the
trying years of the Johnston's Army upheaval and the
cruel misrepresentation of the political misfits sent here
there or thereafter as federal officers, he conducted himself and his affairs always as a wise and forceful leader.

During the closing years of his life he was busy putting the affairs of the Church in order; organizing new
stakes (or ecclesiastic units), in the outlying districts
of the territory; building temples, schools, colleges,
theatres ,and houses of worship. All the needs of man—
physical, mental, moral as well as spiritual—must be
cared for in the true Church of Christ.

After years of incessant activity, much stress, great
accomplishment, some persecution, yet withal deep joy
and satisfaction, his life drew to a peaceful close on
August 29, 1877, in his seventy-seventh year.

A great leader and stalwart pioneer passed to the
Great Beyond!

CHAPTER 16.

THE WISDOM OF BRIGHAM YOUNG

WISDOM may be defined as that condition which results from the proper use of true knowledge. The mere possession of knowledge is not enough and one must use that knowledge for human welfare if one is to possess wisdom. To know God lives is insufficient for we are told that even the devils know God and tremble before Him. Men must be active in doing God's will in order to prove their knowledge and wisdom. A brief review of some of Brigham's teachings may be timely.

One of the secrets of his success is stated by him: "I wish to say that, when I see Elders in Israel who are careless and unconcerned, who trifle away their time, and neglect to attend High Council and other Meetings where there are opportunities to learn, my experience for the best part of forty years teaches me that they never progress—they are as they were, and as they no doubt will be. In my experience I never did let an opportunity pass of getting with the Prophet Joseph and of hearing him speak in public or in private, so that I might draw understanding from the fountain from which he spoke, that I might have it and bring it forth when it was needed. My own experience tells me that the great success with which the Lord has crowned my labors is owing to the fact of applying my heart to wisdom.

"In the days of the Prophet Joseph, such moments were more precious to me than all the wealth of the world. No matter how great my poverty—if I had to borrow meal to feed my wife and children,—I never let an opportunity pass of learning what the Prophet had to impart. This is the secret of the success of your humble servant. I make this application to the Elders of Israel."[1]

"Every time we put forth our ability to do good and build up the kingdom of God, according to the means the Lord bestows upon us, our means and ability will be doubled and trebled. Yes, we shall receive tenfold, and as Joseph said an hundredfold. Have we witnesses of this? Yes, plenty of witnesses. I will mention one little circumstance. When we were finishing the Temple in Nauvoo, the last year of our stay there, I rented a portion of ground in what was called the Church farm, which we afterwards deeded to sister Emma [wife of the martyred Prophet Joseph, who refused to go west with the body of the church.] Brother George D. Grant worked for me then, and planted the corn, sowed the oats; and said this, that, and the other must be attended to. They called for teams to haul for the Temple, and could not get them. Said I, put my team on the Temple, if there is not a kernel of grain raised. I said I would trust in God for the increase, and I had as good corn as there was on the farm, though it was not touched from the time we put the seed in to the time of gathering. I proved the fact. I had faith..[2]

His desire for humility is rather facetiously expressed: "Doubtless many of the Elders think that they are smarter than I am. As Brother Kimball has said, some of the knowing ones marveled when we were called to the Apostleship. It was indeed a mystery to me; but when I considered what consummate blockheads they were, I did not deem it so great a wonder. When they would meet Brother Kimball and myself, their looks expressed, 'What a pity!' Then I would think, You may, perhaps, make tolerable good men after a while; but I guess that you will tumble out by-and-by, just as they

did; they could not stay in the Gospel net, they were
so big and grew so fast; they became larger than the
ship and slid overboard."[3]

He sensed his faults and was ever ready to correct
them: "I am of the opinion that I know and understand
myself, about as well as any person can know and understand me; yet I may think that I know my weaknesses
and incapabilities to the fullest, while others may see
weaknesses that I do not. Still I am so constituted that
when I discover my weaknesses I bear them off as well
as I can; and I say to all people, if you discover that
I falter, when I do the best I can, what are you going
to do about it?"[4]

"I am about as free from what is called jealousy,
as any man that lives; I am not jealous of anybody,
though I know what the feeling is; but it never troubled
me much, even in my younger days. Neither am I sus-
picious of my brethren."[5]

The human side of the man is well expressed by
himself: "We have great reason to be truly thankful that
we are in these mountains. I have said so from the
time we first came here. All we have to do is to do
right, walk humbly before God, deal justly one with
another, and with the whole human family, and let
our worst wish toward our worst enemies be that we
may see the time when they will be obliged to do right.
I never did wish anything worse upon them than they
should do right, pay their debts, deal justly, and walk
humbly one with another."[6]

The cause of the persecution of this people is tersely
stated by him: "They say now that if we will only give
up the doctrine of plurality of wives, they will admit
us as a state, and hail us as a 'pet state,' give us

the preference to all the states, for our industry and prudence.

"But hold on, were we driven into the mountains here for polygamy? Were we driven from York State to Ohio and persecuted and hated for polygamy? No. Was Joseph Smith persecuted and driven from Pennsylvania, with writ after writ, for polygamy? No, * * * * When we were driven from Jackson into Clay, Caldwell and Daviess and other counties, and from there out of the State by the mob, was it for polygamy? By no means. When we were driven from Nauvoo, after having made it like the Garden of Eden, was it because polygamy was offensive to the people? No. * * * * Why was it that we were compelled to leave State after State and ultimately the United States? Because the priesthood of the Son of God is among this people, and they know that if we are let alone we shall convert the world and bring it into subjection to the law of Christ. The devil says, 'I have had power over the earth for six thousand years, and do you think I am going to loose my grasp upon it? No, I will hold it, and before ever the Latter-day Saints obtain one foot of inheritance upon it they will have to contest it inch by inch.' But we will contend with him until we gain power and influence sufficient to convert the world."[7]

The attitude of the people to those not of their faith was usually tolerant and sympathetic. This attitude, naturally, was inspired by the leaders. The following is the testimony of a Mr. Bell (non-Mormon) who was associated with the business firm quoted: "Mr. Bell, of the firm of Livingston, Kinkead, and Co., of Great Salt Lake City, has arrived here within the last few days, direct from Utah. Mr. Bell went out to

Utah with one of the principals of the firm in 1849, for the purpose of establishing business relations with the inhabitants of that Territory. As a community, he represents them honest, sober, and very industrious . . . . Outsiders, or 'Gentiles' have not been subjected to abuse or annoyance on account of negative faith in 'Mormonism.' The troubles between the 'Gentiles' and the 'Mormons' have sprung from meddling, unnecessarily and uncalled for, on the part of the former. Many had come to Utah with the idea that the new faith and 'peculiar institution' were matters which everybody had a right to criticize, talk about, joke about, ridicule, and oppose; and such have invariably got themselves into trouble. Others who have gone there, and who have regarded 'Mormonism' and polygamy as matters pertaining to the 'Mormons,' and attended to their own affairs, have lived in peace and been respected by the community. That a prejudice exists against 'Gentiles' in general is very certain; but it has no practical results, if they mind their own business."[8]

The danger of riches was often stressed by Brigham Young: "This people commenced with nothing. Joseph Smith, the honored instrument in the hands of God to lay the foundation of this work, commenced with nothing; he had neither the wisdom nor the riches of this world. And it is proven to our satisfaction, that when rich men have come into this Church, the Lord has been determined to take their riches from them and make them poor, that all His Saints may learn to obtain that which they possess by faith."[9]

"He [the Prophet] was full of sorrow, trouble, poverty, and distress; but now the people are led into riches by the example, counsel, advice, and dictations of their leaders. They are on the high way to wealth;

and there is danger in it. Here are men that never knew enough of the principles of economy to gather substance or save anything to themselves, until within a few years back; but now they are becoming rich in a moderate point of view. We do not expect to become wealthy like the Rothchilds, or some other large capitalists of Europe. This people are gathering much substance around them, which is a principle of heaven —a principle of Zion, but there is a fear within us lest it cause us to forget our God and our religion. Whether we have much or little, let it be on the altar, for it is all the Lord's whether this people know it or not. Joseph Smith said to this people, that all the wisdom he had was received from the hand of the Lord. All the knowledge, wisdom, economy, and every business transaction pertaining to human life in connection with the spiritual Kingdom of God on the earth, is given unto us as individuals, or as a community, from the liberal hand of God."[10]

"We want this people to become wealthy, but there is an 'if' in the case. If this people can at the same time possess riches and glorify God, then we want them to be rich; but, I would rather see this people half clothed and living in the dens and caves of the earth, than that through riches they should forsake their god."[11]

A religion that is practical made a great appeal to this practical man: "Tradition has taught us that the great purpose of religion is to prepare people to die; that when they have passed through a change of heart, become converted, then they are ready for 'glory' at any moment and to dwell with the Father and the Son in the heavens to all eternity. This is a mistake; for they have to improve, become substantially changed from bad to good, from sin to holiness, here or somewhere else, before they are prepared for the society they anticipate enjoying. They would not be nearly so well prepared for the society of the sanctified in heaven as a person brought up in the lowest class of society would be prepared to present himself properly and conduct himself among the highest and most polished grades of mankind. Those who are counted worthy to dwell with the Father and the Son have previously received an education fitting them for that society; they have been made fully acquainted with every pass-word, token and sign which has enabled them to pass by the porters through the doors into the celestial kingdom."[12]

"I want present salvation. I preach, comparatively, but little about the eternities and Gods, and their wonderful works in eternity; and do not tell who first made them, nor how they were made; for I know nothing about that. Life is for us, and it is for us to receive it today and not wait for the Millennium. Let us take a course to be saved today, and when evening comes, review the acts of the day, repent of our sins, if we have any to repent of, and say our prayers; then we can lie down and sleep in peace until the morning, arise with gratitude to God, commence the labors of another day, and strive to live the whole day to God and nobody else."[13]

A tribute from a non-member of the Church but a friend of national repute is most interesting. In answer to the many critics of Brigham Young, Colonel Thomas L. Kane wrote the following letter to the President of the United States, Millard Fillmore:

MY DEAR PRESIDENT FILLMORE: I have no wish to evade the responsibility of having vouched for the character of Mr. Brigham Young, of Utah, and his fitness for the station he now occupies as Governor of the territory of Utah. I reiterate without reserve, the statement of his excellent capacity, energy and integrity, which I made you prior to his appointment. I am willing to say I volunteered to communicate to you the facts by which I was convinced of his patriotism, and devotion to the interests of the Union. I made no qualification when I assured you of his irreproachable moral character, because I was able to speak of this from my own intimate personal knowledge. . .

It happens felicitously enough for the purpose of accusation before you, that Brigham Young was the man of all others, whose influence carried through that measure with the Church the raising of the Mormon Battalion. It was his American flag that was brought out to float over those hills for the first time; his drums beat, and his brave American speeches rang through the hearts of his people. It was he who said there 'You shall have your battalion at once, if it has to be a class of Elders.' I want you to remark, sir, that this, their first communication with our Government after their expulsion from their homes in Illinois, dates of August 9,1846. 'The best Government on earth.' 'The Constitution of the United States most precious among nations.' This is its language. . .

Young is a hard-working, conscientious, well-tried man. . . Young is fortunate in his family too. I remember him wrapped up in his youngest child, an infant, whose health was suffering from the hardships of the march; and I recollect also that he had a son of the finest promise. Withal, he is so true a fellow, and has so much else to look after—being consulted by his people, as it seemed to me, upon nearly every emergency from an Indian foray to a broken leg or a funeral—that I suspect he pays no manner of heed to any sort of abuse. His wife, however, who comes of a very respectable New England stock, charitable as St. Bridget, and proud of her husband as Queen Victoria, frets, I am told—as pious women will do in such cases—over every fresh piece of nastiness, as if it were an awful and dignified message of Providential chastisement.

During a long attack of malignant fever, from which my constitution has not yet recovered, this lady showed me kindness I can never forget, and you must not wonder that my blood boils to think that upon her, mainly, recoils these brutal slanders.

I have headed this "Personal" rather that I might feel at ease in writing to you in haste, than for any better reason. You are at liberty, therefore, to make what use you please of its contents.

A **final testimony** from the man whose life has just been reviewed will be refreshing. All his life he honored his great file-leader, the modern Prophet Joseph Smith. His words are most impressive. "I honor and revere the name of Joseph Smith. I delight to hear it; I love it. I love his doctrine. What I have received from the Lord, I have received by Joseph Smith; he was the instrument made use of. If I drop him, I must drop these principles; they have not been revealed, declared, or explained by any other man since the days of the Apostles. I feel like shouting hallelujah, all the time, when I think that I ever knew Joseph Smith, the Prophet whom the Lord raised up and ordained, and to whom He gave keys and power to build up the kingdom of God on earth and sustain it. These keys are committed to this people, and we have power to continue the work that Joseph commenced, until everything is prepared for the coming of the Son of Man. This is the business of the Latter-day Saints, and it is all the business we have on hand."[14]

"Were you to ask me how it was that I embraced 'Mormonism,' I should answer, for the simple reason that it embraces all truth in heaven and on earth, in the earth, and in hell, if there be any truth there. There is no truth outside of it; there is no good outside of it; there is no virtue outside of it; there is nothing holy and honorable outside of it; for, wherever these principles are found among all the creations of God, the Gospel of Jesus Christ, and His order and Priesthood, embrace them."[15]

Tribute is here paid also to the many great men and women who as valiant pioneers accomplished the

great work of building this Commonwealth. Without
them the Leader's work had been impotent. No one
recognized that more than did Brigham Young. To them,
one and all, the present generation owes its debt of
gratitude.

A man of the Hour in every sense of the term was
this man Brigham Young. His dynamic energy focused
upon himself every surrounding influence of both good
and evil, light and darkness. Life was to him motion, the
power of growth, progress, development. Concomitantly,
his friends loved and sought his society and counsel
while his enemies hated him and desired his destruction and defeat. Like his revered leader and friend, the
Prophet Joseph Smith, he was the best loved and most
hated man of his day.

It would follow that the last thirty years of his
life and labors would be crowded with action and
clouded by opposition. The founding of cities, towns,
farms, mills, manufactories, schools, colleges, museums,
theatres, halls of science and art, meeting houses, temples,
councils of health, hygenic laws and regulation occupied
his time. These to him spelled happiness and peace.
With these positive forces were mingled the evils which
call for continued resistance. In the years after the California goldseekers came into the Valley were enacted
laws for the prohibition of liquor sale and manufacture;
also against houses of ill fame and gambling dens, which
meant the suppression of vice in all its forms. All of
these needs caused him and the people to undertake
an ever-increasing activity in building righteousness.

The inspiration of God added to his own natural
ability, supplemented by the many-sided and great-souled
men and women leaders by whom he was surrounded,
enabled him to translate with marvelous rapidity his

visions into realities. His fruitful mind was constantly fed with inspiration from his associate leading brethren and sisters whom he loved, respected and counseled with, and who were, like himself, great and mighty men and women whom God had chosen and held in reserve to lay the foundation of His work in latter days. Communal life and the spirit and genius of the Gospel permitted these great men and women to express themselves in all the terms of utility, refinement and spiritual uplift known to mortals. "There were giants in those days!"

No personal praise would Brigham ever accept, nor must we now disparage the greatness of his accomplishment by giving him any undue credit for the great and mighty work of those days. Could he speak to us today he might say, as he so often did while on earth: "Don't give me the credit for our being here or for the work accomplished—it was the result first of an over-ruling Power, who led us every step of the way and who guided our activities after our arrival; also the united effort of all my brethren and sisters. May you do as much for your day in building righteousness on earth, so that our labor may not have been in vain!"

He was in very deed **The Man of the Hour!**

CHAPTER 1:

   1. Brigham Young, *Journal of Discourses*, 6:290.

   2. *Ibid.*, 1:41.

   3. *Ibid.*, 1:41.

CHAPTER 2:

   1. *Journal of Discourses*.

   2. *Ibid.*, 18:247.

   3. *Ibid.*, 6:39.

   4. *Ibid.*, 2:123-124; 4:104; 12:283; 13:215.

   5. *Ibid.*, 8:228; 9:248.

   6. *Utah Genealogical Magazine* 11:110.

   7. Young, *Journal of Discourses*, 5:72-73.

   8. *Utah Genealogical Magazine*, 11:109.

   9. Young, *Journal of Discourses*, 3:91.

  10. *Ibid.*, 1:90.

  11. *Ibid.*, 2:123.

  12. Susa Young Gates and Leah D. Widtsoe, *The Life Story of Young*, p. 22.

  13. *Utah Genealogical Magazine*, 11:110, (J. D. 1:41).

  14. "Autobiography," *Millennial Star*, 25:438.

CHAPTER 3:

   1. Young, *Journal of Discourses*, 14:118.

   2. "Autobiography," *Millennial Star*, 25:438.

   3. *Ibid.*, 25:424.

   4. *Utah Genealogical Magazine*, 11:110.

   5. "Autobiography," *Millennial Star*, 25:439.

   6. Young, *Journal of Discourses*, 1:110; 9:364.

CHAPTER 4:

   1. Joseph Fielding Smith, *Essentials in Church History*, p. 128.

   2. *Ibid.* p. 128.

   3. *Ibid.*, p. 129.

4. "Autobiography," *Millennial Star*, 25:455.

5. *Ibid.*, 25:455.

6. *Ibid.*, 25:487.

7. Young, *Journal of Discourses*, 14:199.

8. *Ibid.*, 8:16.

9. *Ibid.*, 9:331.

CHAPTER 5:

1. Doctrine and Covenants, 110. Also, Joseph Smith, *Documentary History of the Church*, 2:410.

2. B. H. Roberts, *A Comprehensive History of the Church*, 1:398-399.

3. Young, *Journal of Discourses*, 8:189.

4. *Ibid.*, 10:315.

5. *Ibid.*, 3:121.

6. "Autobiography," *Millennial Star*, 25:487.

7. Edward F. Tullidge, *Life of Brigham Young*, p. 83.

8. Young, *Journal of Discourses*, 9:332.

9. "Autobiography," *Millennial Star*, 25:487.

CHAPTER 6:

1. Autobiography, *Millenial Star*, 25:520.

2. *Ibid.*, 25:535.

3. Tullidge, *Life of Brigham Young*, p. 86.

4. *Ibid.*, p. 88.

5. *Ibid.*, p. 89.

6. *Millennial Star*, 21:442.

7. Tullidge, *Life of Brigham Young*, pp. 89-90.

8. "Autobiography," *Millennial Star*, 25:584.

CHAPTER 7:

1. Young, *Journal of Discourses*, 5:97.

2. *Ibid.*, 13:210.

3. *Ibid.*, 5:342-343.

4. *Ibid.*, 7:229.

5. Young, *Journal of Discourses*, 10:20, 328.

6. *Ibid.*, 4:34, 305; 12:170-171.

7. *Ibid.*, 14:149.

8. *Ibid.*, 14:121.

9. *Ibid.*, 14:101.

10. *Ibid.*, 12:229.

11. *Ibid.*, 2:320.

12. *Ibid.*, 5:5.

13. *Ibid.*, 8:181.

14. *Ibid.*, 8:181-182.

15. *Ibid.*, 4:37.

16. *Ibid.*, 2:10.

17. *Ibid.*, 3:123.

CHAPTER 8:

1. Orson F. Whitney, *Life of Heber C. Kimball*, pp. 275-276.

2. Young, *Journal of Discourses*, 4:36-37.

3. Tullidge, *Life of Brigham Young*, p. 95.

4. Young, *Journal of Discourses*, 4:35-36.

5. *Ibid.*, 12:52.

6. *Ibid.*, 2:172, 128.

7. *Ibid.*, 13:211-212.

8. *Ibid.*, 14:80-81.

9. *Ibid.*, 3:1.

10. *Ibid.*, 8:286.

11. *Ibid.*, 2:19.

CHAPTER 9:

1. Tullidge, *Life of Brigham Young*, pp 102-103.

2. Doctrine and Covenants, 107:22, 24; 112:30.

3. *Ibid.*, 124: 108-109.

4. Smith, *Essentials in Church History*, pp. 325, 386.

5. *Ibid.*, p. 386.

6. Edward Henry Anderson, *Life of Brigham Young*, pp. 46-47.

7. Smith, *Documentary History of the Church*, 7:232.

CHAPTER 10:

1. Gates and Widtsoe, *The Life of Brigham Young*, pp. 311-312.

2. B. H. Roberts, *Rise and Fall of Nauvoo*, p. 342.

CHAPTER 11:

1. Young, *Journal of Discourses*, 2:173-175.

2. Frank Alfred Golder, *March of the Mormon Battalion*, p. 30.

3. *Journal History* 13 July, 1846.

4. Smith, *Essentials in Church History*, p. 410.

5. Col. Thomas L. Kane's historical sketch, "The Mormons," printed in Philadelphia in 1850, reprinted in the *Millennial Star*, May 15, 1852.

6. *Woman's Exponent*, Vol. 13. June 1884.

CHAPTER 12:

1. Young, *Journal of Discourses*, 13:85-86.

2. *Journal History*, February 26, 1847.

3. Young, *Journal of Discourses*, 10:307.

4. *Ibid.*, 3:373.

5. Tullidge, *Life of Brigham Young*, p. 443.

6. *Ibid.*, pp. 446-447.

7. Young, *Journal of Discourses*, 9:284; 11:133.

8. *Ibid.*, 10:193.

9. *Ibid.*, 6:172.

10. Gates and Widtsoe, *The Life Story of Brigham Young*, p. 169.

11. Young, *Journal of Discourses*, 10:200.

CHAPTER 13:

1. Young, *Journal of Discourses*, 5:97.

2. *Ibid.*, 3:323.

3. *Ibid.*, 12:286-287.

4. *Ibid.*, 12:93-94.

5. Pearl of Great Price, "Book of Moses," Chapters 6 and 7.

6. Acts 2:44-47.

7. Gates and Widtsoe, *The Life Story of Brigham Young*, pp. 28, 33, 320-356.

8. Young, *Journal of Discourses*, 8:74.

9. *Ibid.*, 12:374.

10. Young, *Journal of Discourses*, 12: 59-61.

11. Edward W. Tullidge, 'History of Salt Lake City," pp| 735, 736.

12. Gates and Widstoe, *The Life Story of Brigham Young*, p. 318.

CHAPTER 14:

1. Young, *Journal of Discourses*, 8:40.

2. *Ibid.*, 16:18.

3. *Ibid.*, 8:40.

4. *Ibid.*, 12:116.

5. *Woman's Exponent*, Vol. 6, No. 13, December 1, 1877.

6. Gates and Widtsoe, *The Life Story of Brigham Young*, p. 298.

7. Young, *Journal of Discourses*, 16:17.

8. *Ibid.*, 12:106-107.

9. Improvement Era, Feb. 1944, pp. 76,77.

CHAPTER 15:

1. Smith,*Essentials in Church History*, pp. 494-510. Also, Gates and Widtsoe, *The Life Story of Brigham Young*, pp. 172-194.

2. *Millennial Star*, 20:470-471.

CHAPTER 16:

1. Young, *Journal of Discourses*, 12:269-270.

2. *Ibid.*, 8:337.

3. *Ibid.*, 8:173.

4. *Ibid.*, 4:21.

5. *Ibid.*, 4:66.

6. *Ibid.*, 8:156.

7. *Ibid.*, 12:272.

8. *Millennial Star*, 20:206-207.

9. Young, *Journal of Discourses*, 2:128.

10. *Ibid.*, 1:78.

11. *Ibid.*, 10:329.

12. *Ibid.*, 10:172.

13. *Ibid.*, 8:124.

14. *Ibid.*, 3:51; 6:279; 13:216.

15. *Ibid.*, 11:213.

INDEX

A

B

C

D

E

W

Y

Z

CPSIA information can be obtained
at www.ICGtesting.com
Printed in the USA
BVHW061716260820
587357BV00003B/145